Both Sides *of the* Mirror

**The Science
and Art
of Ballet**

Second Edition

Anna Paskevska

A Dance Horizons Book

Princeton Book Company, Publishers
Pennington, NJ

Excerpts reprinted with permission of Schirmer Books, a division of Macmillan, Inc., from *Dance Knesiology* by Sally S. Fitt. Copyright © 1988 by Schirmer Books.

A Dance Horizons Book
Princeton Book, Company, Publishers
P.O. Box 57
Pennington, NJ 08534

Cover design and interior design by Anne O'Donnell

Library of Congress Cataloging-in-Publication Data

Paskevska, Anna.
    Both sides of the mirror : the science and art of ballet / Anna Paskevska. —2nd ed.
      p. cm.
    "A Dance Horizons book."
    Includes bibliographical references and index.
    Summary: A technical and artistic discussion of ballet, focusing on its history, physical requirements, exercises, and training.
    ISBN 0-87127-180-X
    1. Ballet dancing—Juvenile literature.   2. Ballet—History—Juvenile literature. [1. Ballet dancing. 2. Ballet—History.] I. Title.
    GV1787.5.P37   1992
    792.8—dc20   92-14804

Both Sides *of*
the Mirror

Also by Anna Paskevska

Ballet: From the First Plié to Mastery,
An Eight-Year Course

It would not be so bad if one could rely upon the teachers, but both in this country [England] and in America, particularly in America, I have come across teachers who have no right to be permitted to teach. They not only fail to teach what is accurate, but in many cases they actually do their pupils grievous bodily harm by giving them exercises entirely unfitted for their age and physique. . . .
We are not machines.

Anna Pavlova

He taught in such a way that the dancer began to know himself more completely, and that, I believe, is the first key to serious work, to becoming an artist—to know oneself, one's gifts, one's limitations, as fully as possible. It is the only way . . . [Pushkin had the ability] to guide the dancer down the right path toward being realistic about his gifts, and then to inspire him to work, and work hard, at making the most artistically of those gifts. He also taught me that no one else can assume this responsibility—an invaluable lesson. He didn't force you, he gave his wisdom freely, and you did with it what you could and would.

Mikhail Baryshnikov
speaking of his teacher,
Alexander Pushkin

Contents

List of Illustrations

Foreword

I was first aware of Anna Paskevska as a very young and very dedicated member of our first English regional ballet company, Western Theatre Ballet, in 1957. She had studied with Olga Preobrajenska in Paris and at our Royal Ballet School. She was seizing every moment of spare time to do intensive classes with Cleo Nordi, the former Pavlova dancer who taught the precepts of that great Russian Nicholas Legat.

This is an impressive pedigree for a dancer and now for a teacher. Anna left the stage for a while after she married, and subsequently she turned to teaching. She has brought to her new vocation the same high seriousness, which is reflected in this book. I am delighted to wish her every success.

Mary Clarke
Editor
The Dancing Times, London

Acknowledgments

I would like to thank Della Cook for her meticulous anatomical drawings; my long ago students Helen Wolfson and Leslie Horn, Helen for her patience in going over the original draft of the manuscript and Leslie for her help with the glossary; Gretchen Warren for her knowledgeable help with the new material; my student Liza Cegles for posing for the new photographs and my colleague Jan Yourist for taking them with such good humor.

Anna Paskevska
1991

Chapter 1

Introduction: A Personal Statement

The science and art of dance cannot be separated. In practice one is indistinguishable from the other. In the studio we unendingly correct details but always with an awareness of the totality of the movement. Dance, like any living art, like any living artist, has a past upon which the present is built. It is a tribute to the wisdom of our masters that dance has matured to today's degree of artistry and technical proficiency.

This book is a reassessment. It attempts to find a balance between the customary and the innovative, between the subjective and the objective, by using both the old tested techniques of classical ballet and some new empirical findings of recent scientific studies.

Like all dancers I am a product of the tradition and evolution in classical dance and I envision my reader as the curious who, while respecting the traditions of our art, is not bound by its mythology, who is still exploring the technique and still discovering personal meaning within the well-known steps. To all dancers their art is a deeply subjective experience, and these prefatory remarks are personal, in reference both to myself and to our common medium, dance.

We who are dancers and teachers of dance are the recipients of the knowledge and vision of our teachers, who themselves were in our position when young. This process of passing down knowledge may be likened to the storyteller's art, which, through tales and myths, preserves and transmits part of our cultural heritage. In many ways the education of classical dancers has been a kind of family affair, at times perhaps even with incestuous undertones. Let us consider some personalities who shaped ballet's tradition; their thoughts have influenced numerous, possibly all, classical dancers and teachers including myself.

In the eighteenth century, dance in the Western world was largely dominated by Italian and French dancers and masters. They traveled extensively, disseminating their knowledge, fostering a uniformity of concepts and terminology, often settling permanently in an adopted country. Towering above all others in the early nineteenth century were two figures, Auguste Vestris (1760–1842) and Carlo Blasis (1797–1878). They heralded and shaped the classical dance we know today. Renowned as the *premier danseur* of Europe in his earlier years, Vestris sustained his reputation as a teacher of great artists and of other teachers. Blasis, however, is now usually regarded as the most important theorist of his century, and his influence has reached well beyond his own classroom; his books on dance theory are still read today. Students of both men transmitted their messages to the next generation.

August Bournonville (1805–1879) came from Copenhagen to Paris to study with Vestris, but his later work with the Royal Danish Ballet and his published manual reflected some of Blasis's theory as well. One of Bournonville's pupils was Sweden's *premier danseur*, Christian Johansson (1817–1903). He took his master's theories to St. Petersburg in 1841. Meanwhile Giovanni Lepri (ca. 1836–1890), a pupil of Blasis, became the teacher of Enrico Cecchetti (1850–1928). Thirty years after Johansson's appointment as ballet master of the Imperial Theatre in St. Petersburg, Cecchetti joined Johansson, assuming the position of second ballet master.

Among the many students of both Johansson and Cecchetti (thus following the parallel lines descending from Vestris and Blasis) were two renowned dancers who later became teachers, Olga Preobrajenskaya (1870–1962), the greatest ballerina of her age, and her frequent partner Nicolas Legat (1869–1937). Olga Preobrajenskaya and Cleo Nordi (1899–1983), Legat's gifted student, were for twenty years the two teachers who most influenced my development as a dancer.

The transmission of our common tradition, which itself has undergone some evolution in its progress, can be illustrated most clearly in a brief family tree.

The philosophy of dance has remained remarkably little changed since the days of Blasis. His advice is still valid, and his principle of good taste governing all aspects of teaching is not only still applicable but surprisingly readable even today. Thus we may say that

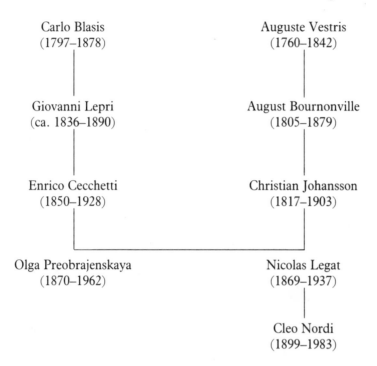

Carlo Blasis
(1797–1878)

Auguste Vestris
(1760–1842)

Giovanni Lepri
(ca. 1836–1890)

August Bournonville
(1805–1879)

Enrico Cecchetti
(1850–1928)

Christian Johansson
(1817–1903)

Olga Preobrajenskaya
(1870–1962)

Nicolas Legat
(1869–1937)

Cleo Nordi
(1899–1983)

one generation passeth away and another generation cometh, but the storytellers of our dance culture have managed to preserve the essence of our heritage.

Since I have no direct knowledge of Johansson's or Legat's method of teaching, it is only by comparing the systems experienced in classes with my teachers that I can draw conclusions about whose method dominated my training. Preo, as Preobrajenskaya was called by all, had an indelible influence, forming an idea of style as she laid the foundation of technique. She taught in Paris from 1923 until 1960. Dancers ranging from the most modest to the world-renowned passed through her studio during those years. In 1946, when I had just come from Moscow to Paris, she took her last class of young beginners, six in all, of whom I was one. After two years we were allowed to take class with more advanced students, although she continued to teach us privately. Eventually we attended the open class and benefited by the example of such accomplished dancers among our classmates as Tamara Toumanova and Rosella Hightower.

In 1949 I was accepted as a *Petit Rat* at the Paris Opera Ballet school, but I attended Preo's classes after school and on Saturdays until

1953. While in many of the basics Preo's sympathies were unconditionally with the old school, her many refinements on the established style and technique made her very much an artist of the twentieth century. Her classes were jewels of clarity in the purest tradition of the old masters, but always there was a deep understanding of each pupil as an individual with individual strengths and weaknesses.*

Nicolas Legat, Preo's contemporary, taught in Russia and later took Cecchetti's place as ballet master of the Diaghilev company. Legat, who was greatly influenced by Johansson, became a theorist of note. He was also the beloved teacher of Cleo Nordi, who studied with him in Russia until the revolution forced her family, like so many others, to flee westward. Nordi danced for several seasons at the Paris Opera before joining Anna Pavlova's company. Later she opened a studio in London, where I studied with her for a decade. (I had already spent a year at the Legat School working principally with Madame Legat, Nicolas's widow, and with Lydia Kyasht, another of Preo's contemporaries at the Imperial School and Maryinsky Theatre.)

Nordi's classes were exacting and precise, challenging the imagination as they strengthened execution. She keenly questioned the reasons behind the accepted modes even as she insisted on the strictest adherence to the classic ideals of form. Her approach bridged the gap between the inherited ideas and their inevitable evolution. It is just such sensitive perception and interpretation as Nordi's which has sustained and enriched classic dance, even as it has in some cases insulated it from the onslaught of the modern world.**

Classic dance is still evolving and changing to reflect the temper and tastes of its environment. It cannot avoid being influenced by the knowledge and techniques that have emerged in this century. It has nevertheless kept a distinctive profile both in the classroom and on stage. The reasons for the relatively constant image of ballet are, I believe, to be found in the technique itself; it creates a body both supple and strong, one capable of interpreting subtle changes of mood or of

*A recent warm biography is *Olga Preobrajenskaya: A Portrait* written by Elvira Roné, Preo's colleague for half a century, who taught some of my classes on those rare occasions when Preo was absent.

**The teaching of Legat is the subject of a recent book by André Eglevsky and John Gregory, *Heritage of a Ballet Master: Nicolas Legat.* Legat was the teacher of Nijinsky, Fokine, Preobrajenskaya, Vaganova, Markova, Massine, Somes, and Nordi, and the Legat book contains the personal recollections of students and such actual Legat classes as were written out by the master or recorded by students. A self-professed teacher of Legat's methods, Mme. Nordi herself continues training dancers and teachers and is currently working on a book on the Legat method.

describing epic events. It is a rigorous, living technique which demands practice and vigilance throughout a dancer's active life. Familiarity with the steps is only the beginning. The class is a daily rediscovery in which each movement must be experienced as if for the first time while being guided by past knowledge.

But what does this process of rediscovery mean to the student and teacher of ballet? A student, especially a beginner, is quite literally at the mercy of the teacher. This awesome responsibility requires that the mentor step back from any subjective idiosyncrasies and perceive the motion in its purest form. Directives and corrections must take into consideration the physical build and capability of the student and relate it to the classical ideal.

Thus it is not enough to know that at the *barre*, *battement tendu* follows *plié*, or that in the center *adagio* precedes *allegro*. The good teacher will continually mediate an intimate yet objective dialogue with the technique and the student. Drawing upon a total familiarity with the technique while recognizing its boundaries, and upon an awareness of the student's talent as well as limitations, the teacher leads the pupil in an exploration. Together they discover the role of gravity and how it serves motion, how intent and gesture are translated into meaning, how physical impulses are balanced to produce a specific shape.

This knowledge is inherent in the daily class, which, if conducted wisely, will not overtax a particular muscle or produce deformities. The development of technique is rather like following a doctor's prescription. Too little medicine will have no effect while too much might make one worse. For example, the often heard classroom injunction to pull up is a call for a necessary postural change which every dancer heeds in the course of training. But some students pull up until they look as if they might topple backward. This not uncommon fault puts enormous pressure on the lumbar area of the spine, inhibits any freedom in the upper body or any expressiveness in the arms, and is painful for the dancer as well as ugly to watch.

Isadora Duncan once said that the skeleton of the classical dancer is deformed. Sometimes, when looking around a classroom, I entirely agree with her statement and sadly reflect that it need not be so. A dancer is a human being first, and as such has to contend with the limitations that physical structure imposes on motion. This last idea is the starting point of this study. I have not attempted to formulate a syllabus or expound a method, though some starting points for both may be found here. What I have attempted is to relate the physiological principles of motion to the basic technique of classical ballet, giving practical advice for attaining optimal proficiency in this *le premier pas* of dance art.

The influences which have shaped my understanding of the balletic art are similar to the experience of countless other dancers of my generation. Many of us can claim Cecchetti and/or Johansson as our grandfather; thus we have direct links with our tradition. Like our distinguished predecessors, we too must be flexible, adaptive, innovative, and receptive to useful information,* but not at the expense of well-tested principles. Without an understanding of these principles, technical evolution will certainly be in danger of corruption for the teacher will not know the reason behind an exercise or how it leads toward a correct execution of other movements. When I see a *battement frappé* executed with a pointed foot, I sense that the teacher must have forgotten, or must never have known, that the flexing on the *cou-de-pied* and the stretching into the extension at the ankle conditions a quick, strong reflex which is essential for all *allegro* movements, especially fast jumps.

Each idea should be accepted or rejected, not on the basis of newness, oldness, or, for that matter, prettiness, but rather on the basis of its contribution to the technique and the art. If the only criterion followed is whether something looks pretty, as in the case of *battement frappé*, then the art of dance is reduced to the level of the purely decorative, and the only evolution we can envision is an endless display of physical prowess. In the hope that dance will survive not only as a sound technique but also as an honest art form, I offer the following pages for consideration. Technique is the language of any art. In the classroom the child learns the language of dance. Some may become poets.

During the ten-odd years since this book was written, dance kinesiology has piqued the interest of scientists and several excellent books have covered the subject. Among them, *Dance Kinesiology* by Sally Fitt and

---

*Much of today's scientific data was unknown even to the teachers of my generation, not to mention their distinguished predecessors; even so recent and generally sound a work as Agrippina Vaganova's *Basic Principles of Classical Ballet* (various editions, 1934–1969) did not have the benefit of much of what we now know about anatomy and physiology. Indeed the scientific study of dance is only beginning, and promising work on the subject is now under way in various places—for example, by Dickinson College physicist Kenneth Laws and Rhonda Rhyman of the University of Waterloo, Ontario. Yet our subject is not unknown to history; as early as 1721, John Weaver had published his *Anatomical and Mechanical Lectures upon Dancing*.

The Physics of Dance by Kenneth Laws (both published by Schirmer Books) provide new and insightful information.

Drawing from these sources as well as others, I have reexamined the information in this work, made a few additions and commentaries, as well as enlarged a couple of chapters to discuss more fully some pertinent material.

Although this book begins with some kinesiological information, it was never my intention that this work should be considered a kinesiological treatise. I have merely sought to disprove the idea held by many modern dance educators that classical dance is injurious by drawing parallels between Dr. Lulu Sweigard's research into what is believed to be good posture and the foundations of classical ballet. In this age of high technical proficiency we can only benefit from the writings and findings of people like Dr. Sweigard. But while recognizing that knowledge of kinesiology and anatomy are essential tools for the teacher and add greatly to the understanding of the student, we must also acknowledge that the scientific language does not lend itself easily to corrections in the studio.

Ms. Fitt rightly remarks that the language used by teachers is more poetry than prose. This observation is supported by the fact that many of the muscles directly responsible for actions cannot be directly felt, like the iliopsoas and the deep rotators of the hip joint. We can, however, infer that they are working when the student's stance is correct and when a movement is performed without compensatory stress. Therefore teachers use images to foster correct execution and often give instructions that seem to contradict the laws of gravity and physics. Yet with these injunctions they enable the student to gain access to hidden resources.

Chapter 2

Physical Requirements

A sculptor works carefully on the armature of his statue, for it will determine the shape of the sculpture. Similarly, the skeletal alignment of a person largely determines the shape of the muscles. The direction of growth can often be predicted by the bone structure of a child. Therefore, aptitude for dance and acceptance into a professional ballet school depend almost entirely on a child's physique.

The teacher examining the child will look for specific proportions and relationships in the skeletal arrangement. The back and legs are checked for straightness; the hip joint is tested for mobility; the shape of the foot is scrutinized for its potential strength (stubby toes and broad feet usually provide more strength and support than long narrow feet).

Classic dance requires a very particular musculature which can be developed through the repetition of the basic exercises. In the years eight through twelve the body is almost totally malleable. Thus the child who is accepted into a professional school or who seriously considers a career as a dancer is forbidden to indulge not only in contact sports for fear of injury but in certain other types of physical activity which may affect the ultimate muscular structure.

The ideal dancer's body is long-limbed. The legs are straight. The feet boast a strong metatarsal arch. The setting of the legs in the hip joint is mobile so that a 180 degree turn-out can eventually be achieved. The pelvis is neither too narrow, which will affect the potential for turn-out, nor too wide, although this is a purely esthetic consideration.

The back is straight and strong. Finally, the head is well shaped and not too large in relation to the rest of the body. The arms, being non-weight-bearing extremities in girls, are shapely and supple. For boys a certain development in the arms is necessary as they must have the strength to lift and carry their partners.* Some weightlifting programs can be beneficial, but those designed to produce bulk should be avoided.

Ligaments must be of normal length, not too tight, not too loose. The double-jointed child has greater difficulty in controlling the shape of motion, while the stiff child may have to use too much force and effort to achieve the desired degree of extension.

Block Man**

The harmony of the skeletal arrangement determines the development of a harmonious musculature. To illustrate this point let us imagine a structure which resembles a person. When the blocks are in perfect alignment, the block person is in no danger of losing its balance. When the blocks are not well aligned, only a deliberate displacement of

*As we know from studies now being done on women athletes, their legs can be proportionately just as strong as men's, while their arms seem to average about half the strength. Because their arms are usually shorter and their shoulders narrower, they have less power and leverage. Also, since female bodies contain less muscle overall than do male bodies (23% for women, 40% for men), women can more easily overload them, causing pain or injury to ligaments and tendons as well as to the muscles themselves.

**These figures, like some others in this chapter, were suggested by illustrations found in the writings of Mabel Elsworth Todd and of Lulu E. Sweigard.

some blocks can keep the structure from collapsing. In the human body it is the muscles which perform the task of adjusting the skeleton to preserve balance. These adjustments create stress and tension, and obviously more force will be needed to keep an unbalanced structure in equilibrium. Very few dancers start off with an ideal body—making it the first concern of the ballet instructor to "place" the student. (See glossary.)

Carlo Blasis in his *Treatise upon the Theory and Practice of the Art of Dancing* (pp. 15–17) divides physiques into two categories to illustrate the problems facing the less-than-perfect body. He distinguishes his categories on the basis of the structure of the legs. Such a distinction was adequate in Blasis's time because the emphasis of dance technique was on the legs. Movement of the body was not extensive and never violent.

Blasis's first category describes the knock-kneed person. When standing in first position this person has space between his heels while his knees are together, because the hamstrings are overlong. To correct this condition the child should stand with the heels together. Although the knees will not *feel* straight in this position, they will nonetheless *appear* straight. Muscles will develop to enforce this position and to provide protection for the knees.

In his second category Blasis describes the bandy-legged person. When standing in first position with the heels together this person has a space between the knees because his hamstrings are too short. Keeping the knees fully stretched will eventually lengthen the hamstrings.

Although it is convenient thus to classify all physiques into two categories, it does not do justice to all the anatomical variables. Because of the nature of contemporary dance, we must examine each section of the body separately and determine how it affects the whole. Some generalizations can, however, be made. Children who are naturally supple have laxer ligaments than stiff children. The former will utilize their suppleness; the latter will work hard to increase their range of motion; yet both will strive to achieve the classical ideal of form.

Each area of the body has a specific range of motion which affects the execution of movement. A too-mobile ankle joint makes the foot prone to supination (rolling out) or pronation (rolling in), which further weakens that area. A tightness in the ankle joint makes the classical pointed foot difficult to achieve. However, daily exercises can increase flexibility and strengthen the longitudinal arch. Similarly, stiffness in the hip joints can be worked out by daily practice, while a high degree of freedom in the hip joint must be constrained to avoid misalignment in the pelvic area. We consider the pelvis again and again throughout these pages, since this section of the body is critical to the correct alignment of one's whole structure.

Each exercise in the classic technique acts on a specific area of the body. For example, *battement tendu* develops the instep and *battement frappé* develops the musculature of the lower leg. Yet beyond this basic consideration, each has the double function of promoting a widening range of motion as well as inhibiting movement that does not conform to the classical shape. The ideal form itself is subject to physiological and kinesiological principles. Classic training, if unwise, can distort. Forcing a young body into shapes for which it is not muscularly prepared can do great damage, not only by causing immediate aches and pains but also by causing long-range displacement and injury.

Early training establishes neuromuscular patterns of response to stimuli. Initially this training is a matter of imitation. The teacher demonstrates, the pupil mimics. Through repetition, neural pathways are created, facilitated by the role of the synapses. As Ms. Fitt writes, "Once a neural pathway has been established, it is difficult to change that pattern of transmission because the neural transmission automatically flows (because of synaptic facilitation) in the established pathway" (*Dance Kinesiology*, pp. 258–259). The habits fostered during this early period form the foundation of later technique; technique not imposed from the outside as our earlier statement "the teacher demonstrates, the pupil mimics" would seem to imply but truly from the inside—the new neural pathways become an integral part of the total vocabulary of motion available to the individual. If the training is sound, the young student may become a pleasing dancer who possesses a harmonious physique and a responsive instrument for artistry. If the training is unsound, the student will develop bad habits which will be reinforced with each lesson and will eventually inhibit further growth. Muscular patterns can become so ingrained that re-education is at best lengthy and painful and at worst impossible. By the time the child is old enough to realize that he/she has been working incorrectly, it may be too late to change.

One of the most common bad habits formed in early training is tucking under the buttocks. An older student I encountered was taught in this fashion. The habit had produced in her, as it would in anyone, enormous thighs and posterior, an increased curvature of the thoracic spine, and strain in the shoulders and neck. Her body maintained equilibrium by extreme muscular contraction and sheer will power. Her muscles had developed such strength that they resisted her attempts to correct her posture and continually pulled her back into her old familiar patterns. To quote Ms. Fitt again: "Changing a motor pattern usually requires a change in the image of movement and giving the central nervous system new information about the desired movement" (*Dance Kinesiology*, p. 259). We began to see some improvement when the student accepted a new sensation—a feeling of sticking out her buttocks; it came as a surprise to her that even when she released the downward and under pull she did not lose her turn-out; on the contrary, it improved. In fact, many movements became easier to perform. Furthermore, she finally realized that although she "felt" that her buttocks were sticking out, in fact they were not. Working with the new sensation, she was able to correct many of her earlier problems.

Classic technique provides the means to acquire a vocabulary of dance at the same time as it builds the musculature necessary to perform the desired movements. It is therefore essential for the instructor to be familiar not only with the series and progression of the standard exercises but also with the modes of execution that individual physique imposes on interpretation. The role of teachers of young students is to forestall a displacement in the skeletal alignment by adequately preparing the young bodies. The exercises must not be beyond their physical capabilities. For instance, a turn-out of 180 degrees is achieved over a period of several years. Little by little the rotation in the hip joint is increased as the connecting muscles gain in strength and flexibility. Flexibility and control must be fostered side by side through all stages of training.

In the next chapter we examine the means for achieving skeletal balance and a harmonious musculature—both of them essential to mastering the art of dance. The next few pages provide diagrams of the bones and muscles discussed in the text.

**COMPLETE
SKELETON**

1 cranium
2 mandible
3 clavicle
4 scapula
  (acromion
  process)
5 humerus
6 sternum
7 radius
8 ulna
9 sacrum
10 innominate
11 femur
12 patella
13 fibula
14 tibia
15 fibula
  (lateral
  malleolus)
16 calcaneus
17 first metatarsal
18 talus

Note: Hand is drawn
supinated (palm up) on
the right, pronated on the
left side of the skeleton.
Left leg is drawn in a
laterally rotated or
turned-out position. This
is a female.

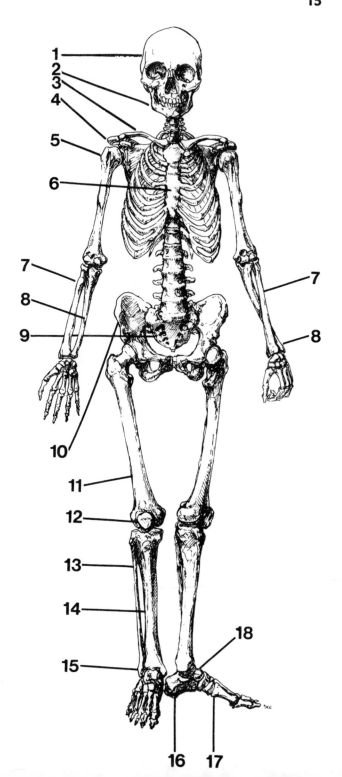

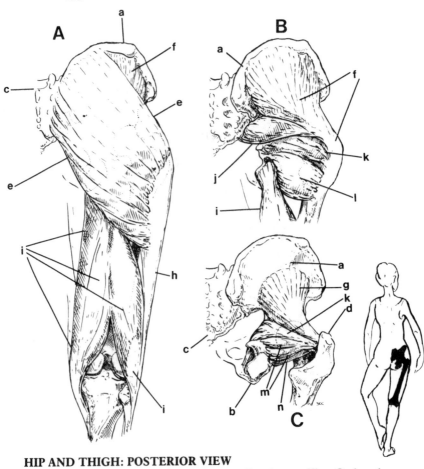

HIP AND THIGH: POSTERIOR VIEW
View A: superficial layer   View B: intermediate layer   View C: deep layer

BONES:
a   innominate
    (ilium)
b   innominate
    (ischium)
c   sacrum
d   femur (greater
    trochanter)

MUSCLES:
gluteus group:
e   gluteus maximus
f   gluteus medius
g   gluteus minimus
h   iliotibial tract
    (g. maximus)
i   hamstrings

deep rotators:
j   piriformis
    (inserts with g. medius)
k   obdurator internus
l   quadratus femoris
m   gemelli interior and
    superior
n   obdurator externus

Note: Drawn in part after J. C. B. Grant, *Grant's Atlas of Anatomy*. Dotted lines
indicate underlying bones.

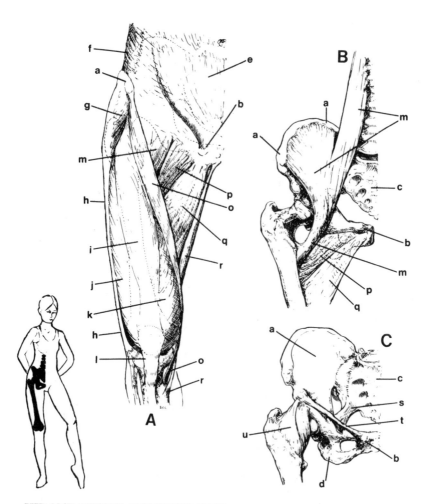

HIP AND THIGH: ANTERIOR VIEW
View A: superficial layer **View B: deep layer** **View C: some important ligaments**

BONES:
a innominate (ilium)
b innominate (pubic tubercle)
c sacrum
d innominate (ischium)

MUSCLES:
e rectus abdominis
f obliquus externus
g tensor faciae latae
h iliotibial tract (t.f.l.)
quadriceps group:
i rectus femoris
j lateral vastus
k medial vastus
l patellar ligament

m iliopsoas
o sartorius
p pectineus
q adductor longus
r gracilis

LIGAMENTS:
l patellar ligament
s sacrotuberous, sacrospinous ligaments
t inguinal ligament
u iliofemoral or Y ligament

Note: Drawn in part after J. C. B. Grant, *Grant's Atlas of Anatomy*, plates 106, 274, 260.

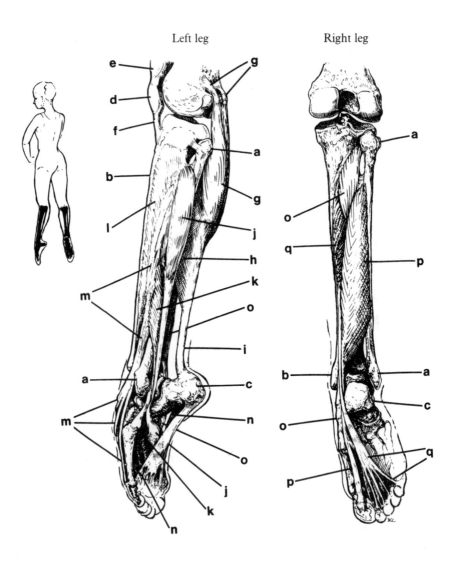

Left leg

Right leg

LEGS
Left leg: lateral aspect   **Right leg: posterior aspect**

BONES: a fibula   c calcaneus
              b tibia   d patella

MUSCLES AND TENDONS:

vastus group: e vastus lateralis
               f patellar tendon
These muscles extend the knee.

gastrocnemius group: g gastrocnemius
                    h soleus
                    i Achilles tendon
These muscles plantar-flex, or extend, the ankle. The gastrocnemius can flex the knee. This group forms the superficial mass of the calf.

peroneus group: j peroneus longus
                k peroneus brevis
These muscles evert the foot, or move the sole of the foot toward the lateral aspect, and maintain the arch when the heel is off the ground.

anterior group: l tibialis anterior
              m extensor digitorum longus
These muscles dorsi-flex the ankle. The extensor digitorum longus extends the toes. Tibialis anterior inverts the foot, or turns the sole of the foot toward the midline of the body.

intrinsic flexors of the foot: n flexor digitorum brevis and
                              plantar aponeurosis
This muscle plantar-flexes the foot and flexes the toes. There are many other intrinsic foot muscles.

deep posterior group: o tibialis posterior
                   p flexor hallucis longus
                   q flexor digitorum longus
This group of muscles plantar-flex the ankle and invert the foot. The flexor hallucis longus and the flexor digitorum longus flex the toes.

Note: Drawn in part after J. C. B. Grant, *Grant's Atlas of Anatomy*, plates 304, 317–320, 328–331.

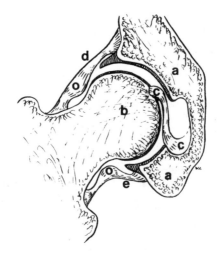

SECTION THROUGH THE HIP JOINT

This is a schematic drawing of a section through the capsule of the hip joint. The joint is in the same position shown in View C of Hip and Thigh: Anterior View.

BONES: a innominate
      b femur
LIGAMENTS: c ligament of the head of femur
      d fibrous capsule: iliofemoral ligament
      e fibrous capsule: ischiofemoral ligament
      o zona orbicularis
The fibrous capsule of the hip joint completely surrounds the head of femur. It is divided into a number of named ligaments. It is constricted around the neck of the femur. This constriction is called the zona orbicularis.
CARTILAGE: cartilagenous portions of the joint capsule are shaded.

Note: Drawn after J. C. B. Grant, *Grant's Atlas of Anatomy*, plate 282; and Warwick and Williams, *Gray's Anatomy*, p. 447.

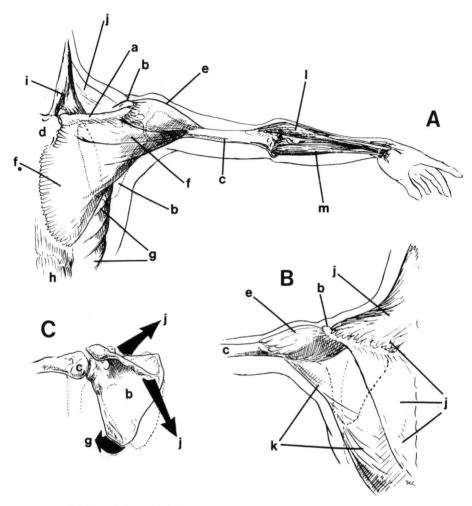

ARM AND SHOULDER
View A: anterior shoulder and forearm   View B: posterior shoulder
View C: rotators of the scapula important in raising the arm: major muscle actions are indicated by arrows, while the resting position of the bones is indicated by dotted lines in this view

BONES:
a clavicle
b scapula
c humerus
d sternum

MUSCLES:
e deltoid
f pectoralis major
g serratus anterior
h rectus abdominis
i sternocleidomastoid
j trapezius
k latissimus dorsi
l brachioradialis, extensor carpi radialis
m flexor carpi radialis

Note: Drawn after J. C. B. Grant, *Grant's Atlas of Anatomy*, plates 13, 23, 24, and MacConaill and Basmajian, *Muscles and Movements*, p. 189.

ARCHES OF THE FOOT

This figure shows the longitudinal and transverse arches of a right foot. Above is the longitudinal arch as seen from the medial side. Below is the transverse arch as seen in the plane of the tarso-metatarsal joints. The cuneiform and cuboid bones are drawn. The arrow above the upper foot indicates the first cuneiform bone, which appears at the right of the lower drawing.

Note: Drawn in part after J. C. B. Grant, *Grant's Atlas of Anatomy*, plate 347, and MacConaill and Basmajian, *Muscles and Movements*, p. 246.

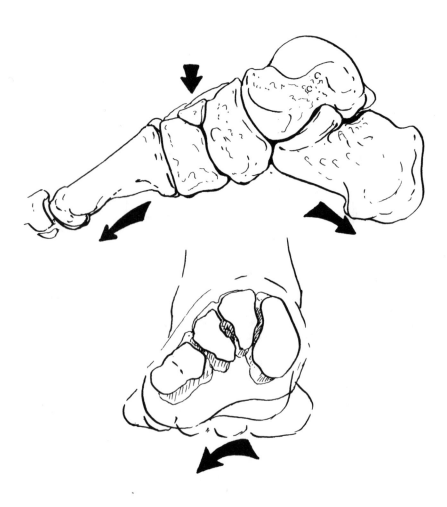

Chapter 3

Posture and Placement

Contrary to the suggestion of some poets and critics, dance does not defy gravity. Rather, it uses gravity as an ally and accomplice, mixing with it a little illusion that the observer may see as magical. The pact with gravity, however, cannot be made unless the body has already proved itself a worthy ally. And illusion is a fickle partner unless technique controls the tricks. So we need to talk about mechanics and consider dance from a purely athletic point of view.

It is not necessary for a dancer to know the names of all the muscles involved in performing a given motion; it is sufficient to be able to recognize a few principles of motion and apply them to classic exercises. But we should appreciate that, in the network of muscles and nerves we know as our body, we have at our disposal a sophisticated machine with levers to lift, extensors to extend, flexors to flex, ligaments to protect the integrity of joints, and a computerlike mind to direct and control all actions.

A runner does not have to remind himself to put one foot in front of the other. When his mind says "run" his muscles respond to the command. A baby taking his first wobbly steps, on the other hand, is not expected to run the next day. He will first have to develop the musculature and motor control needed to perform that more complicated motion. Similarly, through the repetition of standard exercises the beginning student of dance has to establish the musculature and motor control that will be commensurate with the complexity of his art.

Dance exercises utilize the natural function of the body to

formulate a wide variety of movements. Let us consider these functions in their most fundamental terms; later in this chapter several more complex ideas and their appropriate scientific terminology are introduced.

Primarily a limb is either straight or flexed; by going from one to the other we get motion. There are five alternatives inherent in motion which we can relate to dance movements or positions:

1. When both legs are straight, both feet on the floor, we are ready to form the five basic ballet positions.

2. When legs are flexed at the knees, one foot or both feet on the floor, we have *pliés* and preparations for jumps and turns.

3. When one leg is lifted straight out, a variety of *battements* can be executed.

4. When a leg is flexed as it is lifted, all movements derived from *retiré* can be done.

5. When the flex and the straight are combined, all known movements can be produced.

Movement is created by the contraction of specific muscles acting on joints or mechanical levers. But to bring about a specific movement, only a mental picture of the motion is necessary. We need not tell the quadriceps or the deltoids to contract when doing a *battement jeté* or a *port de bras*. These muscles will perform the role desired if they are given a clear command, and the command will be clear if one's mental picture is clear.

The dance student usually forms a mental image of a movement by observing his teacher. He then attempts to reproduce the motion by imitating the visual image he has retained. Although the beginner need not know that the abdominals contract in a *developpé devant*, the teacher should have a precise understanding of muscle function and skeletal relationships in order to make the commands and corrections congenial with physiological and kinesiological principles. This understanding consists of isolating the prime movers, in any given motion, from the muscles which only support the action. It must be based on the scientific laws governing human movement potential.

In any given motion two forces are at work: (1) muscles acting on mechanical levers to produce movement; (2) muscles and ligaments acting on joints to stabilize the structure. For example, in a *developpé devant*, the prime movers act on the leg executing the *developpé*. These include the quadriceps, the sartorius, the tensor fasciae latae, and the six deep rotators which preserve the turn-out. And, once a 90 degree extension has been reached, the iliopsoas comes into play.

All other muscles support and stabilize the structure. Back and abdominal muscles aid the extension by supporting the upper body and thus help keep the alignment. The verticality of the supporting leg, which is stabilized in part by the hip joint ligaments, ensures the correct relationship of the whole body to the line of gravity. If a student contracts his ribs toward the working leg (tensing the thorax unnecessarily), we know that either the leg is not yet strong enough for the height sought or the student is confused about the purely supportive role of the upper body. If allowed to sacrifice correct alignment to high extension, the student will never develop ease of execution.

Each motion, no matter how complex, can be broken down into its essential components. Therefore, we need to return to the five choices stated earlier and to examine a little more closely the points of flexion.

In the shoulder and arm complex we have three major joints: (1) at the shoulder, the humerus in the glenoid cavity; (2) the elbow, connecting the upper arm to the radius and ulna; (3) the wrist, connecting the arm to the hand. The characteristic position of the arm in classic dance requires the long bone of the upper arm, the humerus, to be rotated inward. The rest of the arm is then aligned to form a gentle curve.

The arm should move freely within its shoulder joint, without either a sympathetic lift of the shoulders and scapulae or a contraction in the upper chest. While the neuromuscular reflexes are becoming habitual, care should be taken to keep the back and chest muscles smooth (not voluntarily contracted), so that the action of the humerus is isolated and the joint is uninhibited by opposing contractors.

In the lower extremities there are again three major joints: (1) the hip joint, linked by the femur to the knee; (2) the knee, connecting the thigh to the tibia and fibula; (3) the ankle, connecting the leg to the talus and foot bones.

The femoral head in the hip joint has a lesser degree of rotation than the humerus in its cavity. It is held rotated outward by the six deep outward rotators of the joint (the gluteus maximus is not the only enforcer of the turn-out and in most instances should not be contracted voluntarily). Flexion of the thigh is effected by muscles of the pelvis (the iliopsoas, like the deep rotators, cannot be felt, and must therefore be taken on faith). The sartorius stabilizes both hip and knee. Extension of the leg above a certain height, dependent on the individual physique, involves a tilt in the pelvic area. But in heights below 25 degrees the pelvis should always keep its level alignment.

The flexion and extension of the foot are controlled by the numerous muscles of the calf: the extensor digitorum longus and the extensor hallucis longus on the anterior side; and the peroneus longus and gastrocnemius on the posterior side, to name only two pairs. Some muscles control the outward rotation of the foot, some the inward rotation; some also act as stabilizers, and many are flexors as well. (See Wells and Luttgens, *Kinesiology,* p.187.) The foot should not initially be forced outward. It should remain aligned with the knee, whose position is in turn conditioned by the degree of rotation in the hip joint.

Just as flexibility of the arm is increased by using it independently of the shoulder, so the flexibility of the hip joint is increased by working it without displacing the pelvis. These two joints are active in an aggressive way; that is, they initiate movement and carry it through. The torso, pelvis, and head are engaged passively; they support and respond.

This last statement may be misleading. In the early stages of learning the student will begin to isolate and localize movement. The leg is lifted without a contraction of the rib cage. The arm is held without lifting the shoulder. But the ultimate purpose of the isolation is to enable all parts to harmonize and cooperate.

A muscle will pass through a cycle of active, passive, active, in a matter of moments during the course of a movement. For example, in a *battement frappé,* while the foot is flexed on the *cou-de-pied,* the tibialis anterior is contracted; tension is released as the foot points and the knee straightens; the muscle contracts again to flex the foot as it returns to the *cou-de-pied.* The tibialis anterior can be seen and felt in its contraction, but many other muscles that are unseen and unfelt are actively or supportively contributing to the movement.

Mabel Elsworth Todd succinctly states, "Only as bones are aligned for proper function can muscles be relieved of unnecessary work" (*The Hidden You,* p. 222). Muscles develop commensurately with the demands made upon them. If excessive force is required to maintain equilibrium, and yet more force is needed to move the joints, then muscles are performing double duty. In a balanced and efficient structure minimal force is used to maintain equilibrium. Thus correct alignment facilitates all motion and safeguards against an unattractive, overdeveloped musculature.

Classic training alters or redefines some skeletal relationships in specific ways, and these changes facilitate the kinds of motion dancers have to perform. But dancers, like everyone else, are subject to physical laws; their technical accomplishments are also governed by the rules of human movement potential and rely on subcortical impulses to motivate action.

Dr. Lulu Sweigard, who has written extensively on the subject of skeletal alignment, conducted a study on about 200 students. It was designed to test the importance of the subcortical patterning of muscle function on the actual mechanical function of the skeleton. She discovered that changes in skeletal alignment could be achieved through the use of mental images to locate and visualize movement in the body.

Although the method described by Dr. Sweigard did not involve muscle response or development, the changes in posture resulting from the application of her ideokinetic (mental picturing) technique are precisely the areas where a change of alignment occurs in a well-trained dancer. She categorized these changes into "lines-of-movement," and these lines are so central to our discussion that for

Lines of Movement

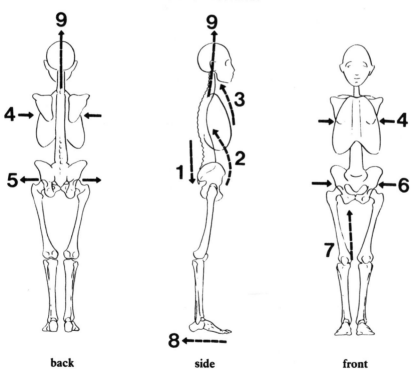

back   side   front

clarity as well as for future reference, we cite pertinent excerpts from each. A line of movement should be thought of as the direction or way in which a change occurs in some particular bodily alignment; as such, it can be likened to a grammar that underlies the vocabulary of dance.

1. *A line-of-movement to lengthen the spine downward.* . . . The anteroposterior tilt of the pelvis decreased, and in doing so it lowered the level of support of the spine. Thus, one of the directions of movement in the spine as a whole was downward as the response to imagined movement's having released tightness in the muscles of the back, especially in the lumbar area.

2. *A line-of-movement to shorten the distance between the mid-front of the pelvis and the twelfth thoracic vertebra.* As a result of posture teaching, the front of the pelvis moved upward and the twelfth thoracic vertebra moved forward, shortening the distance between them. Various mechanical, structural, and functional factors support this change as contributing to more efficient support of weight, as follows: (a) the relative location of the sacral table and the femoral heads; (b) the transfer of weight forward, downward, and outward from the sacral table through the pelvis to the acetabulae and femoral heads; (c) the function of the iliofemoral ligaments on the front of the femoral joints; and (d) the location of the psoas major muscles, whose shortening can influence both the balance of the lumbar spine, in the form of a forward curve, and the position of the front of the pelvis between the lumbar spine and the proximal femora.

3. *A line-of-movement from the top of the sternum to the top of the spine.* The changes which indicated the need for this line-of-movement were increase in the length of the spine, increase in the sitting and standing heights, backward movement of both the first thoracic vertebra and the head, and upward movement of the breast bone.

4. *A line-of-movement to narrow the rib-case.* The decrease in the width and circumference of the rib-case and the lowering of the position of the shoulders indicate that less muscular effort is put forth in "holding" either the chest or shoulders in position. . . . Success in this line-of-movement makes a marked contribution to alignment of the spine for weight support, to flexibility of the shoulder girdle, and to a more efficient position of the pelvis and lower limbs.

5. *A line-of-movement to widen across the back of the pelvis.* The fact that all patterns of normal movement of the lower limbs begin at the femoral joint indicates the great importance of the stability and mobility of this joint, both for weight support and for movement. The position of the heads of the femora in their sockets is as

important to the efficiency of their mechanical function as the position of the hub of a wheel on its axle is to its mechanical function. When muscles across the back of the pelvis are constantly tighter than necessary, the heads of the femora cannot be centered in their sockets; and their movement, especially that of flexion, meets strong muscular resistance.

This line-of-movement helps to release the tightness of the outward rotators of the femora which so often occurs when the ribs are held upward (the lifted chest) and the anteroposterior tilt of the pelvis is too marked. . . . it *does not* increase the horizontal width of the pelvis—as most students postulate when first exposed to this line-of-movement.

6. *A line-of-movement to narrow across the front of the pelvis.* This line-of-movement improves muscle control on the inside of the thigh joints and thus contributes to the centering of weight in the femoral joints. Whereas the preceding line-of-movement released muscle tightness on the back of the pelvis, this one promotes an increase of muscle work on the inside and front of the femoral joints, which helps to prevent weight from sagging against the Y ligaments. Even though these ligaments are the strongest in the body, when they are subjected to persistent stretching stress they will eventually lose their ability to return to normal length when such stress is removed.

The muscles whose activity is increased by this line-of-movement are probably the psoas major, the iliacus, the pectineus, and the adductor brevis and longus on each side of the body.

7. *A line-of-movement from the center of the knee to the center of the femoral joint.* The change of the lower limbs toward a vertical position for support of the pelvis indicates an improved relationship of the femora to the pelvis at the femoral sockets. . . .

Only when the lower limb is controlled close to the pelvis can it engage in its synergy of movement with minimal strain placed on the joints of the knee, ankle, and foot. Success in this line-of-movement below the pelvis is as important in promoting change of the pelvis toward a more efficient position as is success in the line-of-movement above the pelvis to narrow the rib-case. In other words, the alignment of structures above and below the pelvis necessarily influences the balance of the pelvis itself.

8. *A line-of-movement from the big toe to the heel.* . . . This, with decreased tilt of the pelvis and better control of the femora close to the pelvis, results in a more centered weight thrust at the ankle joints, less pronation and eversion of the feet, and hence reduction of the inside length of the feet.

9. *A line-of-movement to lengthen the central axis of the trunk upward.*

Since all changes in the position of the skeletal parts ultimately contribute to a lengthening of the central axis of the trunk, this line-of-movement is one which promotes many simultaneous changes in the trunk, especially in the alignment of the spine and the position of the head, as the student gains experience with other lines-of-movement. Furthermore, it supports the concept of centered control of both the balance and the movement of the body as a whole. The stability of an imagined central axis can exert indirectly a strong influence on the efficient performance of all patterns of movement in any activity. If the dancer, for example, wishes to bend laterally as far as possible, he invariably will bend farther without muscular strain by thinking of bending the central axis instead of trying to thrust his ribs sideways. . . . (Sweigard, *Human Movement Potential*, pp. 193–196.)

Dr. Sweigard proved the possibility of changing the alignment, not through muscular rehabilitation but through changes in subcortical impulses. This study would support the notion that a dancer's idea of shape is as powerful a force for change as is the muscular action used to produce motion. In their daily class dancers consciously manipulate bones to produce specific shapes; subconsciously they are repatterning subcortical impulses so that the shape of the motion complies with the image they have formed. That image must be based not only on some historic or cultural idea of beauty but on sound physiological principles as well. Both the ability to cope with increasingly complex steps and the musculature to perform these steps are acquired progressively. Areas of sensation are created, and the student begins to *feel* what is right: The shape fits the image. These processes cannot be hurried or forced. If a child attempts movements beyond his mental and physical capacities, muscle stress is likely to upset the delicate skeletal balance. Incorrect training can result in potentially dangerous alterations of physical balance. It is therefore necessary to consider the relationship between the artistic technique and the human machine.

Alignment from the Classic Point of View

Good posture begins with the alignment of the spine. The spine can be compared to an obelisk like Cleopatra's Needle or that pillar of chiseled stone known as the Washington Monument. The sacrum forms the base, and each subsequent vertebra depends for its alignment on the one beneath as well as the one above. At the top of the column, the atlantoaxial articulation acts as a fulcrum which balances the mass of the head. Below the neck, the shoulder–arm complex hangs by its muscular attachments to the spine. This can be likened to the wooden water-carriers still seen in parts of Eastern Europe.

The sacrum is attached to the pelvic girdle at the sacroiliac articulation. It consists of three bones (which fuse into two at puberty): the ilium, ischium, and pubis. Compare the pelvis to a bowl with the rim higher in the back than in the front. It is supported by two poles (the legs) which are attached at an angle, rather than being neatly vertical. This strange structure is hardly functional in terms of movement, but it has one thing in common with the human skeletal structure: if the bowl or pelvis dips, tilts, or is otherwise displaced, the rest of the structure has to alter its shape in order to maintain equilibrium.

Skeletal Alignment

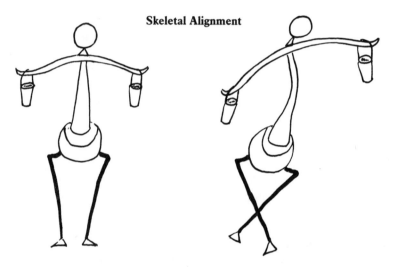

Each section of the body is worked two ways: one to increase mobility and the other to increase control. Each ligament that has been stretched beyond its normal length has to be reinforced by an increase in the strength of the muscles of that area. If the muscles are not strengthened, unwanted displacement of the skeleton will occur.

Correct Posture

The head is balanced on the atlantoaxial articulation like a ball on a fulcrum, or like a ball on the tip of the nose of a performing seal. The chin is at a right angle to the spine, ensuring the verticality of cervical vertebrae.

The shoulder–arm complex is anchored in front to the sternum and clavicle, in the back by muscular connections to the spine. The sternum is uplifted as in the third line of movement described by Dr. Sweigard. This uplift is essential both to the strength and to the mobility of the upper body.

The clavicles are held back to achieve a full opening of the upper chest. This action also enables the scapulae to lie flat against the back. The rib cage is narrowed as in Sweigard's fourth line of movement. This position of the upper body provides support for the shoulders and arms so that they feel independent and balanced.

To describe the pelvic position let us reconsider the image of the bowl. The bowl must not tip either forward or backward but must balance perfectly on its supports. The weight of the pelvis must not be allowed to sag onto the hip joints. This position requires a complex adjustment and is described by Dr. Sweigard in the first, second, fifth, and sixth lines of movement. Adjustment consists of lifting the front of the pelvis, which shortens the distance between the pubis and the twelfth thoracic vertebra and lengthens the spine downward (not to be confused with "tucking under"), decreasing the tension in the lumbar area. These movements contribute to placing the pelvis in a balanced position on top of the femoral heads. Such a position also preserves the integrity of the hip joint ligaments.

Rotation of the femoral head in the hip socket often results in a pronation of the feet and therefore puts stress on knee ligaments. To counteract this tendency it is important to implement the seventh line of movement. For the dancer this involves a greater awareness of the role the inner thigh plays in all motion.

Feet are aligned to the degree of rotation in the hip socket; weight must be evenly distributed between the inside and the outside of the foot. Proper weight distribution produces the eighth line of movement. This position protects the lower limbs from injury resulting from jumps.

The total effect of the series of realignment is one of lengthening through the central axis, standing tall and light, as described in Sweigard's ninth line of movement. In classic dance these changes in alignment are established slowly through muscular development. Inherent in these adjustments is the danger of displacement.

Role of Muscles in Alignment and Common Faults

The shoulder–arm complex has a wide range of movement, for, unlike the pelvic girdle, the shoulders can act independently of each other. To a great extent freedom of movement in the shoulders and arms depends on the position of the thoracic spine and ribs. Tension in the rib cage is often transmitted upward, resulting in contracted shoulders, protruded scapulae, and decreased mobility in the arms.

The arms must retain their freedom to be fully expressive. This freedom is ensured by the centered position of the upper body discussed earlier. The humerus is rotated slightly inward to achieve the curved look of the classic arm (the point of the elbow is held up and points back when the arm is in second position); the rotation of the humerus lifts the elbow. The lower arm is rotated in opposition (outward); the wrist is aligned with the elbow and should neither droop nor flex backward.

Because almost all arm movements are executed with the help of the back, shoulder, and pectoral muscles, no voluntary tensing of one particular muscle is necessary. The deltoids especially must be used without stress. They are powerful abductors and rotators, but if overworked may develop undesired bulk, especially in female dancers. Given the number of upper torso muscles contributing to arm movement, it is superfluous to contract one with more force than another. Once the humerus has been rotated each muscle naturally assumes its role of holding the arm in place.

Tension in the upper torso because of involuntary and unnecessary muscle contraction is generally the result of faulty alignment farther down the line. The cause of the tension may be a tilt of the pelvis, transmitted to the upper body by a curvature in the spine. If the tilt is forward the spinal adjustment will throw the ribs out, forcing the shoulders to pull back and the head to poke forward. If the tilt is backward (tucking under of the buttocks), it will cause a depression of the rib cage. A dancer will then tend to overcompensate for the curvature by forcing the shoulders upward and back and thrusting the chin up. There is also a tendency to lean (sideward contraction of the rib cage), in *adagio*, toward the working leg. This not only spoils the line of the *développé*, but it also prevents the correct development of the extension, for the deep muscles of trunk and leg will not be used efficiently.

Dr. Sweigard's third and fourth lines of movement give the dancer a characteristic uplifted and open position of the upper body. With some dancers this uplift has led to a common distortion whereby the thoracic spine acquires an overextended backward tilt. Thrusting the ribs upward and forward thereby creates an enlargement of the rib cage and puts an enormous amount of pressure on the lower thoracic and upper lumbar areas. And the damage does not stop there. It affects the whole body all the way to the feet, causing stress on the ligaments which can result in permanent injury.

Abdominal muscles and the deep muscles of the spine control the elongation of the torso, keeping the thorax's weight off the lower extremities and the pelvis. This line of movement is number nine in Dr. Sweigard's categories. If for a moment we can forget our original

Opposing Forces

image of Cleopatra's Needle as representative of the spine, and substitute a picture of a chain hanging from a ring and weighted down by a heavy ball, we will have a more dynamic idea of the opposing forces at work.

The ring exerts an upward pull on the chain, lengthening it upward; the ball exerts a downward pull on the chain, lengthening it downward. In the human body the downward force is exerted by gravity and the weight of the limbs themselves, while the upward force is exerted by the muscles. When the skeletal structure is correctly aligned, the muscular tension necessary to hold it upright diminishes. For a dancer this means that more strength is available to execute the motions, since less strength is diverted to keep the equilibrium. When this uplifted stance becomes habit, the ribs become free of tension. Unhindered breathing can then serve the dancer in phrasing and in conserving energy.

The rectus abdominis connects the rib cage to the pelvis. It is active in keeping the lower back straight and in preventing unnecessary tension from creeping into the upper chest and inhibiting the freedom of shoulders and arms. The firmness of that muscle determines the firmness of the waist. Control in that area in the female will allow the male dancer to manipulate her in supported *adagio*. Yet the firmness must not result in stiffness. The body must be pliable and responsive. Rigid control is useless.

Pelvic Alignment

The pelvis determines the correct alignment of the rest of the body. It holds the half-way position between one's lower and upper halves, and redirects the weight of the upper body. Any displacement in that area affects the spinal column and therefore the alignment of the whole structure.

Envision again our image of the pelvis as a bowl. Its centeredness is dependent upon the first and second lines of movement: a decrease in the anteroposterior tilt of the pelvis lengthens the muscles of the back, while a shortening of the distance between the mid-front of the pelvis and the twelfth thoracic vertebra ensures the efficiency of the psoas major by placing it in a favorable position to act and to support the more superficial muscles in abduction and flexion. The position of the pelvis can be determined by the position of the anterior superior iliac spine, which must face straight out with neither a forward nor a backward tilt. This region corresponds to the place on our bowl where the high back curves to become the lower front. For all muscles to be totally effective, the pelvis must be properly aligned before movement begins.

Correct alignment of the pelvis lengthens the sacral spine, which then releases the tightness in the muscles of the lumbar area and straightens the lumbar and thoracic curvatures. This is why dancers appear to have such straight backs. Support for this position comes as much from the deep muscles of the spine as from the abdominals and superficial muscles of the back. The effectiveness of the musculature depends on the relationship of the outer walls of the abdomen to the axis. If we view the pelvic structure from above and imagine it to be a bicycle wheel, we can envision spokes connecting the central hub to the rim of the wheel. The spokes are of equal length, each exerting the same amount of force toward the center. If several spokes are broken on the same side, the connecting tension will be broken and the wheel will become unbalanced. In our living structure the abdominals, which form one side of the rim of the wheel, press toward the spinal column—that is, toward the wheel's hub. The pelvis is now positioned effectively to maintain the verticality of the spine. It follows that correct placement of the pelvis and verticality of the spine relieve the abdominals from excessive tension.

The most common fault in the pelvic area is the backward tilt of the pelvic bowl, a condition almost always caused by tucking in the buttocks. This stance, similar to that of a fashion model, overextends the hip joint ligaments by displacing the femoral head in the acetabulum. The consequences of this displacement are far-reaching.

Displacement of the femora has a devastating effect on the whole body. In the lower half, the thigh muscles are made to work twice as hard as necessary because the iliopsoas is no longer in a position conducive to optimal flexion. Consequently, the thighs become large and bulky. The knee ligaments are overstretched and can no longer protect the knees from injury. Owing to the angle at which the weight is borne by the ankle, the feet are pushed into pronation. In the upper half of the body, the spine adjusts to this tilt in the pelvis by increasing curvatures. The whole structure is now held by intense muscular contraction. Imposition of specific shapes on an unbalanced structure precludes ease of execution. Thus expression, characterization, and fluidity of motion are all beyond the range of dancers who have developed techniques that contradict their skeletal alignment.

Turn-out

Perhaps the most distinguishing feature of a classic dancer is the turn-out. The celebrated and important turn-out is effected primarily by the six deep rotators which form a muscle group behind the hip joint. Although the gluteus maximus is often contracted in enforcing a turn-out, its role is greatly exaggerated. To test this fact, stand with your feet in parallel position and slowly open the toes to first position. Now consciously relax the buttocks. While the gluteus maximus may have contracted when the rotation was in progress, once you are in position such contraction is no longer necessary to hold the turn-out.

The deep rotators assume the duty of holding the turn-out; yet if allowed, the gluteus maximus will deny the deep rotators the role they are designed to fulfill. Since we cannot feel them at work, it is easy to ignore the rotators' function and to rely on superficial muscles which can be felt to contract, such as the gluteus maximus. A main problem with contracting any muscle beyond its functional need is that it grows with use, and a large posterior has never made a better dancer.

The rotation of the femoral head in the hip socket necessitates an adjustment of one's total weight around the axis. A dancer cannot afford to carry all the weight on the heels. It must be shifted forward over the longitudinal arches. This shift makes the rise onto half and full pointe possible and ensures the verticality of all jumps as well as safe landings. The degree of rotation in the hip joint determines the degree of turn-out of the feet. That rotation is transmitted through the femur into the knee, and through the tibia into the ankle. The relationship of femur, knee, ankle, and foot remains the same as when the feet are parallel, and the whole complex rotates as one.

However, the ankle joint is capable of a further rotation outward without jeopardizing the alignment of the leg. This extra rotation is taught when the student has established a correct rotation in the hip joint after a few years of study and allows the dancer to assume a "perfect" fifth position. It must be noted that when the dancer faces directions other than the front, the turn-out is judged in relation to the dancer's alignment and not in terms of the audience. In other words, the dancer will present to the audience different planes of the body when the choreography is other than frontal. This plasticity of the body in space viewed from different perspectives is what makes dance interesting. Moreover, there are positions in the classical technique that allow the supporting leg to be angled closer to a 45-degree turn-out than to a 90-degree. This positioning is used in first *arabesque* on *pointe* for greater stability and in *pirouettes en arabesque*.

Knees and Feet

The knee is extremely vulnerable to injury. If it is not strictly aligned to the rotation of the femur, the ligaments which stabilize the knees will be stretched and lose their ability to protect. One's knee should never be forced outward without the supportive alignment of the foot, nor should it be allowed to fall inward while the foot is forced outward.

The young student should begin with a 45-degree turn-out position. Rotation will be gradually increased as the network of enforcing muscles is developed by the exercises at the *barre*. The foot will eventually be allowed to seek a greater degree of turn-out by an outward rotation at the ankle joint, but not before the muscles of the area can resist pronation. Keeping the turn-out at a 45-degree angle also helps to place the body weight centrally over the longitudinal arches.

Numerous muscles of the calf and foot flex, rotate, and stabilize, and are used in varying degrees to enforce one's alignment. An even distribution of weight between the inside and the outside of the foot is essential to the proper development of the musculature of the lower leg and the protection of the knee ligaments. The foot retains its relationship to the ankle without distortion. To force a turn-out in the foot while the femoral head is not adequately rotated is like hitching a horse to the rear of the buggy and then expecting it to push instead of pull. The result of forcing is a weakening of the ankle joint; the foot responds to this stress by rolling inward (pronation); the arches drop, further weakening the potential strength of the foot.

When pointing the foot it is helpful to put more emphasis on the stretch through the big toe. Because most people have more flexibility on the outside of the foot than on the inside, it is necessary to counteract the tendency to sickle by inhibiting the stretch on the outside and emphasizing it on the inside. In some respects it is misleading even to say that we point our toes; the pointing is done by the extension of the ankle and the contraction of the longitudinal arch, which shortens the distance between the metatarsals and the calcaneus (heel). The toes themselves stretch and thus provide a gentle curve from the ankle downward that gracefully finishes the line of the leg.

We have indicated some dangers inherent in faulty alignment. It must be remembered that any displacement will affect the whole body, either directly on the joint where the displacement occurs or indirectly as compensation for the misalignment. When one area of the body is out of alignment, balance is restored by some compensatory muscular action. In physically taxing activities like dance, these compensations result in stress and overdeveloped musculature. A muscle under continued stress begins to respond in a neurotic way. The dancer may experience cramps, trembling, loss of elasticity. She may become muscle-bound, or resort to compulsive activity such as contracting the shoulders when jumping or sticking out her chin and tensing her neck muscles in an *adagio*. The stress may be transferred to the hands and wrists, which become stiff and inexpressive. All these are symptoms of basic misalignment and cannot be corrected until the cause is found.

As is repeatedly stressed in these pages, any striving for

equilibrium in an unbalanced structure puts enormous stress on the musculature. The harm that can be done to the skeletal harmony cannot be overemphasized. Any deviation from good posture limits the effectiveness of the whole body—the dancer's instrument—and may even cause serious injury. But classical training is harmful and distorting *only* when it disregards the natural relationship of muscles and bones in the human anatomy.

The teacher of young students especially must know how far he can push a student. Particularly in the case of talented youngsters, the teacher must realize that allowing them to do movements for which their bodies have not yet developed enough may ultimately prevent the full flowering of their talent. Such movements are likely to develop an ungainly musculature because of faulty skeletal alignment, and these results may in turn become so fixed that correction is never achieved.

The first three years of training establish the placement upon which the mature dancer will rely. At this time all exercises should be performed in their simplest form, without taxing either the extension or the stamina of the child. Stretching exercises should always be done in conjunction with strengthening exercises. The height of an extension should not be stressed; rather, it should be restricted to 90 degrees or lower. Such restriction is conducive to three major good habits: a correct stance on the supporting leg without overextension of the hip joint ligaments; a correct process of unfolding or lifting the leg without undue stress on the quadriceps; and the correct "square" placement of the pelvic bowl.

The pelvic area and the rib cage are probably the most obvious areas of misalignment as well as the most critical for the future well-being of the body. Maybe the injunction "pull up" should be replaced by "press in." Children usually pull up by sticking out their ribs. As discussed earlier, this causes stress in the upper lumbar and lower thoracic areas of the spine. It also displaces the center of gravity, thus creating compensating strain in other areas of the body. It is precisely because a young body is almost totally malleable that care should be taken not to destroy the natural relationship of joints to bones; thereby one will protect the ligaments and ensure that the muscular development keeps pace with the demands made by the technique.

Let me end this discussion with the wise words of Mabel Elsworth Todd: "The action of all centering muscles works for economy of control in that no effort is being wasted by holding parts out of alignment, that is, away from center" (*The Thinking Body*, p. 203).

Chapter 4

Progression of Training

Because dance is a living art, its evolution is inevitable. Each new generation of dancers and teachers leaves its mark on the technique in the form of innovations or adaptations without, however, altering the basic character of classical ballet. For more than a hundred years the structure of the ballet class has remained unchanged and the development of a dancer within the structure of the technique has also followed traditional forms. We may wonder at such constancy, but I suspect that as long as children grow and develop at a predictable rate we will continue to use the technique in that traditional manner.

That is not to say that dancers today perform in the same fashion they did a hundred or even fifty years ago. Our technical range has greatly increased, yet the preparation for this extended range needs still to follow certain conservative paths. No matter how sophisticated we become in the application of the technique, there can be no shortcuts in the education of a dancer.

The process of dance education is a long one and cannot be hurried regardless of the aptitude of the student; furthermore, the art form must be viewed in its totality throughout the training period lest one aspect of development gets overemphasized. Throughout that process a subtle balance is maintained between increasing the range of motion and preserving the balanced relationship of one part of the body to another. In the early years of training the physical ability of a child depends as much on the stage of physical development as on any inherent talent. By avoiding overtaxing this ability one also avoids creating areas of stress that lead to unwanted and often unsightly musculature. Working hard does not mean straining. On the contrary, it requires understanding just how much effort is needed for a particular motion and learning how to isolate the prime movers from the supporting areas. For example, a child should not be urged to lift the leg so high that she/he sacrifices placement, a straight back, an aligned pelvis and a stress-free shoulder girdle. The strength to lift the leg will develop with the years, and the process will benefit from attention to placement since the correct muscles will be used from the onset.

Traditionally the balletic technique is viewed by both dancers and teachers as painful. It is often believed that if one is not hurting, one is not working hard enough. "No pain, no gain" is a favorite axiom of the proponents of this philosophy. While it is indisputable that a certain degree of discomfort accompanies dance training, it is essential for reasons of health that a dancer be able to distinguish between necessary discomfort and repeated overtaxing of muscles in the belief that only then one is really working hard. There is a fine line dividing "enough" from "too much." Admittedly, there is no movement without tension, but it is equally true that there is no movement possible when joints are locked; trying to move a joint that is being forcibly held is both ungainly and inefficient. Indeed, a most important aspect of dance training resides in the acquired ability to move limbs without locking the joints.

Although a great deal of attention has focused on the "athletic" properties of ballet, the claim is more a valuable marketing tool than a useful concept for dancers and it needs to be defined. Stronger and bigger muscles do not make better dancers. Dance is motion; a muscle-bound body moves with effort, its range is circumscribed.

The emphasis on the development of muscular strength has also led some teachers to promote the use of a contraction of the inner thigh when the leg is brought back from an extended position as in a *battement tendu* —the muscles of the inner thigh are contracted for the return to fifth. The action in itself may seem innocuous, and students like it because it makes them feel as if they are really working hard as they labor to bring the leg back to fifth. But this action has a devastating side effect. By contracting the inner thigh, one reverses the flow of energy; instead of lengthening the musculature and sending the energy into the floor as the heels lower, it reverses the flow upward toward the crotch.

The implications of such a reversal are numerous. It prevents the dancer from making full contact with the floor after landing from a jump. It affects a logical use of the *demi plié* both at the outset and the end of a jump or any movement that includes a *relevé*. (The *demi plié* is designed to provide the body with a mechanism that works like a spring coil; like a pogo stick, the *demi plié* has the ability to give the spring necessary for a jump as well as absorb the shock of landing.) By programming such a reversal into the neuromuscular response, one undermines the smooth transition from one position/step to another without adding any real benefits to the technical ability of the dancer.

Ballet training is divided into very distinct phases. In early training, control and strength are emphasized to gain the correct stance as well as train the muscles to respond in a very specialized way. Through this stage the big muscle groups of the body are shaped and worked, like the quadriceps, the gluteus group, and the gastrocnemius as well as the muscles of the torso.

The most important aspect of early training is establishing correct placement through the execution of the basic exercises. Avoiding areas of stress is achieved by progressing through the vocabulary at a pace that is in harmony with the physical development of the child. During that period the technique is presented in a most straightforward, perhaps austere, way, without embellishments or superficial mannerisms. The good habits that are established will enable the student to successfully integrate later challenges. Because our children start dance at such an early age, this elementary period is lengthy. However, whether a child starts at six or eight years of age, the intermediate level will not be reached until the age eleven or twelve. By that age they will stand correctly in a full fifth position (180 degrees), will be able to maintain turn-out in extensions to 90 degrees, and will know the four different basic jumps—*soubresaut, changement assemblé, sissonne, petit* and *grand jeté*—as well as *pas de chat*, to cite the most basic. They will also know the connecting steps like *pas de bourrée, glissade* and *failli*.

Additionally, they will have practiced spotting from their first year of study, moving on to *chaînés* in their second or third year as well as *pirouettes en dehors* in that third year. In the fourth year *pirouettes en dedans* will be introduced.

Lastly, the concept of *épaulement* needs to be included from the second year as an intrinsic part of training. At this stage it is taught without an emphasis on the spiralling action described earlier, but as positions of the body, head, and arms in relationship to the front. Cecchetti's descriptions of these positions are wonderful at this introductory level.

Having established a measure of control through the strength of the outer musculature, the way is open to begin to internalize the effort required for movement. Although the acquisition of strength is still a primary concern, it is tempered by the idea that inner musculature, although not physically felt, is in fact supporting as well as actively working to produce movement. At this intermediate stage relinquishing overt physicality is an all-important concern. Through reliance on the inner musculature the dancer begins to develop the long muscles characteristic of the technique; performance of the vocabulary begins to acquire ease and fluidity. From a strong center the dancer can reach beyond limitations toward a wider, freer range of motion. The concept of isolation also acquires a deeper meaning. This concept, mentioned earlier as the ability to move a part of the body without involving another and most important without locking the joint that is to be moved, is best illustrated by the *petit battement sur le cou de pied* exercise. In this movement the working leg is held at a 45 degree angle to permit the foot to rest on the ankle. The hip joint is stabilized, it does not move; the position of the working foot is similarly stable—it does not change the degree of flexion; meanwhile the knee joint is totally free to perform the beating, in and out action of the *petit battement*. The correct execution of this exercise relies on the ability to hold both the hip joint and ankle joint in position while the knee joint performs all the action. All ballet movements involve a degree of isolation; the process of learning the technique moves the students from the obvious to the very subtle application of this concept.

Similarly, the concept of *épaulement* can now be experienced in its full range with a strong spiralling action of the upper back as practiced in the Legat system. This motion enhances and facilitates weight transference which also becomes a subtle form of controlling and directing all motions.

Like the previous elementary stage of training, the process at the intermediate level takes about four years. In all likelihood dancers having reached this level of proficiency will already be performing, but they must be aware that their training is not yet completed. The daily class, if taken with the awareness that technique is still in the process of being refined, its subtleties still in the process of being perfected, will promote further discovery. If the dancer becomes content with repetition, regarding the lesson as a mere instrument of maintaining the level of proficiency or worse, simply a means of warming up the body, then exploration and revelation are left out of the process and both the dancer and the dance are demeaned.

The daily class serves several purposes besides warming up the body for rehearsal. In performance, alignment and academic correctness are often sacrificed for specific effects demanded by choreographers; class serves to realign the body and keep the execution of the classical steps honest—true to their form. But it can also be the place where risk taking can be explored. A myriad of subtleties are possible in the execution of the technique; the dancer reaches into a deep source of knowledge in order to transcend the merely correct execution. Through a leap of faith and a letting go of overt control, the dancer will find the hidden resources that make dance exciting. The performance is raised from competence to greatness and has the power to move and elate.

The training of the dancer can be compared to the discipline of Zen. Daisetz Suzuki, in his book *Zen and Japanese Culture* (Princeton University Press, 1959), describes the training in the art of swordsmanship as comprised of three stages—the stage of Innocence, when the neophyte is ignorant of the implication of that which he is learning, the stage of Affect, when the mind controls every move which makes for a deliberate and uninspired execution, and the final stage of "no-mind", which we may call transcendence, when the technique learned during the first two stages is forgotten to allow the motions to flow freely, unimpeded by analysis and criticism. Anna Pavlova said it very succinctly: "Master technique and then forget it and be natural."

While this idea is ultimately applicable to performance, the state of "no-mind" or transcendence can also be experienced in the studio where it frees the mind to address any number of concerns beyond the purely utilitarian. Minute adjustment can then be made that enhance intent, dynamics, force and fluidity. Then the breadth of the technique can at last be fully, kinetically understood and fully shared with the audience.

Chapter 5

Sequence of a Ballet Class

A strict tradition governs the structure of a ballet class. It is a tradition based on logic, trial and error, and natural evolution. It is unlikely that the lords and ladies at the European courts prepared themselves for their balls and masques with arduous exercises, although they may have flexed their knees or even kicked their feet while waiting for their *entrée*. But they probably did practice some of the steps they were to perform.

When professional dancers made their appearance, generally toward the end of the seventeenth century, feats of technical agility multiplied. These professionals, besides being influenced by the vocabulary of the court dances, dipped freely into the tumbler's and acrobat's repertory. Warm-up exercises mimicked the movements that would constitute the dance itself. Although the early masters did not write down the exercises used as a preparation for dance, we can surmise that some sort of standard warm-up was used by the time the School of Dancing opened under royal decree in Paris in 1661.

Evidence of a sophisticated technique, prior to 1820, can be found by implication in descriptions of actual dances. Between 1820 and 1857 Carlo Blasis (1797–1878) published four books which described the then contemporary and somewhat established technique. These documents were the first to deal with some particular aspects of dance training, and they have formed the basis of subsequent theory.

August Bournonville (1805–1879) established a syllabus which had a very restricted circulation, limited initially to his special audience,

47

his own pupils. The syllabus remained the exclusive fare of Danish dancers until 1951, when Vera Volkova (1904–1975) introduced the Russian system into the school. The Bournonville style and philosophy were taken to Russia by Christian Johansson (1817–1903), who taught in St. Petersbûrg from 1860 until his death. Although Johansson's influence in forming the classic style is undisputed, it is undoubtedly Enrico Cecchetti who stands out as the best known theorist in modern times. Cecchetti's disciples, Beaumont and Idzikowski, codified and categorized ballet training in a systematic way that had not been attempted since Blasis.

Their clear-sighted analysis, as well as the straightforward descriptions in their *Manual*, has perhaps no parallel in the literature of dance. But dance, possibly more than most disciplines, relies on individual influences to shape its form. Classic dance, as taught throughout the world today, doubtless is something of a mixture of these various theories and an application of the experiences of all the great masters: Noverre, Blasis, Bournonville, Johansson, Cecchetti, Petipa, Legat, Vaganova, and a host of lesser known but nevertheless important figures who have enriched the tradition while honoring the classic form.

In the classroom the living tradition is experienced anew by the participants; the daily ritual cannot but be influenced by today's perceptions and advanced physiological discoveries. Yet the purpose of the class remains the same. This purpose is threefold. (1) It warms the muscles so that the execution of physically taxing movements becomes less hazardous. (2) It shapes the muscular development and conditions the mind to give commands of ever increasing complexity. (3) It prepares the dancer to respond to the demands of choreographers. The daily class is essential even for accomplished dancers, for they too must constantly re-examine and refine their technique. Like a fine musical instrument, the body needs to be tuned to keep its tone.

The sequence of the *barre* exercises is based on a logical development and gradual involvement of the entire body; it forms the basis of the classic technique. The logic of the sequence is almost mathematically precise in its influence on muscular development. Each exercise not only warms the muscles but establishes areas of sensations which prepare the body for the next exercise. Cumulatively, the exercises condition the dancer for all possible moves encountered in center work. A comprehensive *barre* is the alphabet without which no word, let alone sentence, can be formulated. Center work tests the validity of the experience at the *barre*. Without any artificial support the dancer must reproduce the sensations and shapes just experienced at the

barre, then apply this knowledge to execute *adagio* and *allegro enchaîne-*
ments.

In more specific terms, *barre* exercises help to increase mobility
in the joints, to strengthen the muscles, and to establish control and
coordination. Class begins with *pliés* because of the centering and
general warming properties of this exercise. Then *battements tendus* are
given as the first controlled stretching. *Battements jetés* take the leg just
off the floor in an action similar to the previous exercise, but they
introduce a new dynamic component with the thrown quality of the
motion.

Battements fondus gently unfold the leg, testing the mobility in
the hip joint while the placement of the pelvis is preserved. *Ronds de*
jambe par terre explore the rotation of the femoral head within the hip
socket. *Battements frappés* strengthen the ankle and the foot. *Ronds de*
jambe en l'air introduce a rotary movement in the knee while strengthening the whole leg. *Développés* increase both control and extension while
preparing for sustained work in the center.

Petits battements isolate and enforce a sustained outward
rotation of the femoral head and prepare for the execution of all beaten
steps in the center. *Grands battements* utilize all the knowledge gathered
from the previous exercises in a strong upward thrust. *Grands battements*
are sometimes done after *pliés* as the second exercise. This practice is a
vestige of the sequencing described by Blasis, and it may have worked
at the time when an average of forty-eight *pliés* began the class. No doubt
it is also mainly responsible for the overlarge thighs of some Italian and
French ballerinas.* A more gradual warm-up, favored today, warms the
muscles thoroughly before attempting the more strenuous exercises.

A Cecchetti *barre* finishes with small jumps facing the support;
the Russian method favors *cambré* with *port de bras,* while the French
emphasize extension with stretching exercises with one leg on the *barre.*
A well-balanced *barre* should not exhaust any one particular area of the
body. Exhaustion will result in a series of compensating tensions and
destroy the harmony of the work.

Having completed the exercises at the *barre,* the dancer repeats
some of them in the center. But if every exercise were repeated in the
center the class would be enormously long. The teacher therefore selects
certain exercises and combines them into sequences to test balance or
aplomb. The variations are limitless. For example, a *port de bras*

---

*Although *grands battements* have been blamed for overdeveloped thighs, the
number of *pliés* preceding them could also be the cause for the malformation.

sequence, which begins center practice, could incorporate *temps liés* with *pirouettes*, or *pas de basque* with *grand port de bras*. *Battements tendus, battements jetés, pas de bourrées*, and *glissades* go well together; *battements frappés, petits battements, ronds de jambe par terre* and *en l'air* linked by *pas de basque, soutenue en tournant*, or *pas de bourrée* are also compatible. In advanced classes *pirouettes* can be part of any sequence. Beginners would practice *pirouettes* in a separate, simpler sequence by quarter turns, halves, and finally a complete spin. Each exercise selected to form part of an *enchaînement* should be executed cleanly before it is incorporated into a sequence.

Center *barre* is followed by an *adagio* which can be repeated four or even six times. It is always better to repeat an exercise rather than to move on to something else without first having assimilated the previous information. Four or five *enchaînements* of *allegro* follow, in progressive gradation of height and difficulty. The girls next put on *pointe* shoes. Boys practice high beats or *tours en l'air*. The class ends with a series of *petite batterie, grands battements*, and of course the traditional *révérence*.

Although the sequence of the class is unvarying, the variations on its standardized theme are endless. The specific selection will depend upon the level of the class and the particular focus of the teacher on any given day. It may even depend on a concept introduced on a Monday which is developed, amplified, and explored in all its applications during the remainder of the week. Thus the pupil can experience all that is implied by the concept as it is applied to different steps. Although a week is sufficient time to understand an idea intellectually, it takes much longer to correct a fault or to assimilate totally a new concept. Every dancer has experienced the slow process of re-education of the neuromuscular system and the accompanying muscular development when a bad habit has been diagnosed and corrective measures are taken.

Because it is ultimately much easier to learn correctly than to unlearn, the young dancer is led carefully, step by step. He learns to control and direct his movements, discovering his limitations and his strengths, until they comply with the principles of the classic technique. Ultimately, he can enjoy the freedom the technique has given him, and he can dance. Consider Blasis's warning—"A bad habit once acquired is almost impossible to eradicate"; but also realize that good habits are equally persistent. Correctness is, therefore, well worth any added time and effort required initially.

Learning to dance is very much like building a house. At the outset there must be a concept of what is being built. The foundation is laid; then the skeletal framework of the house is erected. Thus the final shape of the house is anticipated. The quality of the wiring and plumbing will influence the efficiency of the structure. The choice of decorations can enhance the overall style or can be a distraction. The best dancers, like the most beautiful houses, should begin with a sound structure and then rise and take form within the ideals of three inseparable concepts: function, efficiency, and beauty.

In the next chapter the ten standard *barre* exercises are described, including the manner in which they prepare the dancer for work in the center.

Chapter 6

Barre Work

Anna Roje, who became one of [Legat's] favorite pupils, tells how, upon arrival at his studio as an established ballerina from Zagreb, she was not permitted to dance in his class. He would not allow her to execute a single enchaînement, *but insisted upon her doing only* barre-work *for six months, until her faults and placing were remedied. He insisted upon correct beginnings.*

—André Eglevsky and John Gregory
Heritage of a Ballet Master: Nicholas Legat

If we believe, with Mme. Vaganova, that the whole wisdom of classical dancing is revealed in the study of jumps, then we must seek the source of that wisdom in the exercises that lead to *allegro;* that is, in that modus operandi of dancers known universally as the *barre.*

The *barre* is not simply a warm-up for center. If it were, then jogging around the room for ten minutes would accomplish the same end less painfully. *Barre* exercises have far greater significance and hold a central place in the formation of the dancer. Performed in their logical order, the ten exercises condition, prepare, and anticipate the execution of essentially all movements of the classical vocabulary. Each exercise works a specific body-area, but it also involves the rest of the body in a supporting capacity. Thus the pelvis, because it is central to equilibrium, is strengthened with each exercise; the shoulder girdle learns how to cope with stress generated by the legs; and the arms gain mobility in the shoulder socket while being molded into a particular shape.

A dancer's placement at the *barre* will determine his placement in the center. Execution of steps in the center is similarly influenced by the correct execution of exercises at the *barre*. Feet, ankles, knees, and hip joints have each a specific range of motion; this range is either expanded or limited by the type of action classical dance demands. Most problems in execution that are encountered in center work can best be corrected at their source: during *barre*. In fact, most problems originate from poor execution at that critical period of the class.

Most exercises fulfill more than one function, even though they may work one body area more specifically than another. Thus *pliés* center the body; during their execution a dancer finds the place to which he has to return for equilibrium or for total vertical alignment. Feet get particular attention during *battements tendus, jetés,* and *frappés*. The hip joint area is exercised in a variety of ways with *ronds de jambe par terre, fondus, petits battements, développés, ronds de jambe en l'air,* and *grands battements*. Knees are strengthened with the execution of *battements frappés* and *ronds de jambe en l'air*. The wisdom of the *barre* inheres in that not one area is overworked before another area is tackled. When we look at the sequence of the exercises, we realize that their order is as inevitable as their number.

Cleo Nordi often remarked during class that classical dance is as precise as mathematical equations. With this thought, let us now proceed to examine each exercise in detail.

Pliés

Plié is the first exercise of the *barre*. In executing a *plié* the body's alignment is experienced in relation to the outward rotation in the hip joint. This is perhaps the chief physiological experience of this exercise. In all positions the pelvis remains centered, so that the line of gravity falls between the feet in second and fourth positions and falls over the feet in first, third, and fifth positions. The knees remain poised over the feet throughout the bending and stretching. The weight of the body is equally distributed during the action.

In second and fourth *ouverte* the feet are placed about eighteen inches apart (or the dancer's foot length and a half). These positions provide a precise feeling of isolation of the sartorius muscle which helps keep the knee aligned to the rotation in the hip joint. In both of these positions the heels remain on the floor throughout. In first, third, fourth *croisée*, and fifth positions the heels are allowed to come off the floor when the depth of the *demi-plié* has been reached. After the descent is completed and the ascent begins, the heels regain contact with the floor as soon as the achilles tendon allows it. Heels lift only in response to the depth of the *plié*, this is not a movement in itself. The placement of the pelvis and the turn-out of the legs make this lifting off inevitable when the achilles tendon has reached its full stretch.

The action in all positions is continuous: ascension begins as soon as the depth of the *plié* has been reached. In the closed positions the passage through the *demi-plié* should not be emphasized, but rather the action should continue smoothly as the heels lift off or as they regain contact with the floor. The bending of the knees should be felt to be supported by the posterior muscles of the thighs, while the quadriceps are not voluntarily contracted. Thus the hamstrings support the descent, while in the ascent they should be drawn together (or toward each other in the open positions). Awareness of the role of the hamstrings prevents the quadriceps from overexerting themselves during the ascension. The posterior muscles of the legs are both stretched and strengthened in this exercise.

The benefit of the *plié*, however, is not only in its stretching properties, but also in its power of rebound. If the muscles are tightly contracted there can be no rebound but only two separate impulses: one to produce the downward movement and the other to produce the upward thrust. If the *plié* is allowed to be divided into descent and ascent the continuity of the motion is destroyed and the muscles work twice as hard as necessary. Overdeveloped thighs can be the result of this manner of executing the motion. Even in the most gentle and controlled descent the potential for a powerful rebound can be experienced.

The placement of the pelvis is never sacrificed to the depth of the *plié*. It remains in place, as do the shoulders, head, and the whole upper torso. The rotation in the hip joint is isolated and monitored for constancy during motion; this experience can be a reference point for all other motion.

In executing the *plié* it is helpful to exhale during the descent and to inhale during the ascent. Rhythmic breathing will minimize the tension generated by the motion. Tension is of course to some extent an inevitable component of any movement. But dancers learn early how to control it in order to facilitate motion; forced tension only inhibits the natural movement of the joints by producing a contraction in the area of action.

The fluidity of all motion depends upon the efficiency of the *plié*. This fluidity is first experienced at the *barre*. In the center, a good *plié* does not necessarily mean a deep *plié*—it is good because it serves exactly the movement that follows. An *entrechat quatre* requires a shallower *plié* than does an *entrechat six*. The power of the *plié* resides in its ability to rebound: the dancer bends the knees only so far as the next step warrants, then extends the limbs in a strong push against the floor. This extension can be slow and gradual if a sustained *adagio* is performed, or it can be a sudden quick thrust in *allegro enchaînements*, but without the *plié* almost nothing can happen in dance. In landing, a centered *plié* softens the impact of the jump and guards the joints and muscles against injury.

Pliés stretch and strengthen the musculature of the legs. At the *barre* they establish the degree of rotation in the hip socket and develop the muscles to preserve that outward rotation while the body is in motion. They place the body in relation to the line of gravity and anticipate the action of all jumps.

Battements Tendus

Battement tendu is as basic to the classic vocabulary as the *plié*. Whenever a leg disengages from a closed position the mechanics of *tendu* (stretched) come into play. The weight remains on the supporting leg when the working leg stretches out, and the toes never lose contact with the floor. *Tendu* can be executed in all directions. The body remains *en face* for *tendu* to the front, side, and back, and it assumes the appropriate *épaulement* for *tendu* in the *croisé*, *écarté*, and *effacé* positions.

The impulse for the motion comes from the top of the leg. One's energy is sent through the leg into the heel and then into the toes. The weight, at the outset, is on both feet, and it shifts onto the supporting leg as soon as the working leg begins its outward stretch. Although there is no weight on the working leg, contact with the floor is preserved as the leg extends, first through the ball of the foot, then through the toes. This action is reversed on the return to fifth position. The shift of weight is subtle, hardly perceptible, yet critical to the correct transfer of weight in later, more complex, exercises. Each time the working leg returns to fifth position, the body's weight is shifted again to two feet. Because the action of the working leg is isolated in the hip socket, any motion of the pelvis is excluded. The closing and opening of the working leg does not affect the basic placement of the pelvis; it remains level throughout the action, allowing a constant rotation of the femoral head in the hip socket.

Battement tendu has many variations. It can be done with a *demi-plié* when the leg returns to fifth (the knees generally straighten before the next *tendu* begins); or it can be executed with a *demi-plié* on the supporting leg at the moment of extension (*battement soutenu*). In this case, the *demi-plié* involves only the supporting leg, the working one remaining straight throughout. This *battement* can also end with a rise onto *demi-pointe* when the working leg returns to fifth position. The rise to *demi-pointe* is onto both feet with the weight evenly distributed between them. Weight distribution becomes critical when *soutenu en tournant* is introduced in center practice. The turn in that step is a swivel on both feet; therefore, the correct execution of *battement soutenu* will logically lead to the correct execution of the *pas* in the center.

Battement tendu can also be divided into two parts with a *dropping* of the working heel into fourth or second position, followed by a *raising* of the heel (*relevé*) before the leg returns to fifth. This can be executed with a *demi-plié* or with straight knees in the open position; in both cases care should be taken to keep the weight even between the two feet so that the line of gravity falls equidistantly between them. The sequence of transfer of weight should be as follows: (1) weight on both feet in fifth position, prior to the extension; (2) weight on supporting leg when the working leg is stretched to *pointe tendue;* (3) weight even between the two legs as working heel is brought down to the floor; (4) weight on supporting leg as the toes point again; (5) weight on two feet when the working leg has returned to fifth.

Several faults can occur when this exercise is done with straight knees. One tendency is to drop all the weight onto the working leg when the heel is dropped; another is attempting to keep all the weight on the supporting side. Both faults cause a displacement in the pelvic area. Either can be easily avoided if the dropping of the heel is accompanied not only by a shift of weight but also by a lengthening of the posterior leg muscles right down to the heel. This lengthening helps to place the weight evenly between the two legs. When the foot points again, the dancer's attention should remain focused on the extension of the posterior leg muscles in order to counteract a lift of the hip on the working side.

Correct execution of the transfer back and forth from the supporting leg conditions the body to assume a good stance in all preparations for *pirouettes* as well as for quick shifts of weight in *allegro* combinations. The direct influence of this exercise can be seen in center work with *temps liés, glissade, soutenue, pas de basque, tombé,* and *balancé.* In each of these steps, the relatively gentle disengagement of one leg from a closed position is a major component of its whole movement.

Battement tendu strengthens the whole leg, increases the mobility of the instep and the strength of the ankle, and establishes the floor contact essential for the push-off action of most *allegro* steps.

Battements Jetés

Jeter means "to throw." This *battement* borrows its essential character from an object thrown in the air. The thrower controls the action and determines the quality of the energy invested at the outset. The leg can be thrown in any direction, but in *jeté* it is no higher than 25 degrees. Then, following the simple rule that what goes up must come down, it returns to the closed position. Both legs are straight, and the toes of the working leg are fully pointed as soon as it leaves the floor.

Battement jeté is often described as an extension of *battement tendu* with the toes leaving the floor at the end of the full opening. While this explanation is technically correct, it disregards the dynamic idea of throwing which is inherently part of this movement. The exercise is variously termed by different schools as *battement dégagé*, or *tendu jeté*, or *battement glissé*. Each term, while describing part of the movement, adds nothing to the quality of energy conferred by the word *jeté*. Consider: *Dégagé* (i.e., disengage) only deals with the opening of one leg, a disengagement of one limb away from the other. *Tendu jeté* (stretch throw) is almost contradictory in its imagery—compare putting a book on a table to throwing it down. The two actions are quite different in intent as well as in the quality of energy involved. *Glissé* refers to a sliding relationship between the foot and the floor. This action is part of the *battement*, but it does not describe the movement in its entirety. The beauty of *battement jeté* is in the dynamism of the outward thrust of the working leg, which, having reached its predetermined height, is allowed to return to its original closed position without a further contraction of the thigh muscles. One impulse controls the execution and lends the *battement* an air of freedom.

As in the previous exercise, the action in a *battement jeté* is localized so that the thrust of the leg does not affect the placement of the pelvis. In all directions, the turn-out established in fifth position must be preserved. It is all too easy to lose the turn-out during the opening of the leg. If it is lost, when the foot returns to fifth position the heel and toes must be pushed back to close the fifth correctly, and this extra motion is often accompanied by a wiggle of the pelvis. The student who has lost control of the turn-out during the thrusting out of the leg has to rely on the leverage provided by the floor to re-establish it. It can be assumed that the muscles of the hip joint which control the turn-out are not working, the foot and pelvic wiggles being merely symptoms of this inactivity.

If a student is allowed to persist with this type of execution, he will not develop the strength and control which this exercise is meant to engender. Furthermore, he will become susceptible to injuries of the knee and ankle by encouraging an incorrect alignment of the leg muscles. The remedy is to gradually develop the strength in the hip joint so that the muscles of that area are active at all times. The turn-out established in the first two exercises, in *plié* and *battement tendu*, is further reinforced in this one. The rotation of the femoral head is coupled with a slightly higher flexion, increasing the mobility in the hip joint within a controlled extension.

There are a few variations of the basic *battement jeté*. It can end with a *demi-plié* on both feet, or it can involve a *demi-plié* while the leg is out with a momentary hold in the open position. It can also be done *en cloche* or *balancé*, the leg swinging from front to back passing through the first position. In intermediate and advanced classes *battement raccourci* can complement a *jeté* combination. The *raccourci*, as its name implies, shortens the limb: After the initial thrust outward, the leg bends at the knee and the foot is brought to the *cou-de-pied*, *devant* or *derrière*, before closing in fifth position, with or without a *demi-plié*.*

Because of its dynamic nature, *battement jeté* prepares for the correct execution of many *allegro* steps. Every time a leg opens in a strong straight extension, the mechanics of *battement jeté* come into play. It influences directly the execution of *assemblé*, *petit jeté*, and *petite cabriole*. The initial thrust for *pas de basque sauté* and *saut de basque en tournant* is also derived from this exercise.

Battements Fondus

Battement fondu is a controlled extension and flexion of both legs. After doing a *dégagé* to second position as a preparation, the working foot is placed on the *cou-de-pied;* the supporting leg does a *demi-plié;* as the supporting leg stretches, the working leg extends to a *pointe tendue* or to an angle of 15 to 90 degrees. The working leg then returns to the *cou-de-pied* as the supporting leg melts into *demi-plié* in preparation for the next extension.

---

*Although not a variation on the theme, *retiré passé* is often introduced in a sequence of *battement jeté*. The working leg bends as the toes are brought up to knee height of the supporting leg. No displacement occurs in the pelvis and a good outward rotation is preserved in the hip joint during flexion. The *retiré passé* anticipates the position necessary for *pirouettes* and for the action of *pas de chat*, *temps de cuisses*, *tour piqué*, and *temps levé sur le cou-de-pied*.

The feeling of the *fondu,* as its name indicates, is one of soft melting and stretching. The movement can be compared to taffy being stretched and folded by a candy maker. This is a placement exercise *par excellence.* The dancer experiences the correctly placed relationship between leg and body throughout the gradual unfolding of the leg to the desired height. The pelvic area remains stable except when the movement is done *derrière;* a slight tilting forward over the hip joint is then allowed if the leg rises above an angle of 15 degrees. (The tilt is dependent on the height of the leg: the higher the leg, the more pronounced the tilt.) No "sitting" or sinking down onto the hip joint of the supporting side is allowed, as it would result in a displacement of the pelvic bowl. On the side of the working leg, turn-out is explored and enforced through the gradations of the height to which the leg extends.

In the Italian and French schools this exercise is always taught with the toes pointed. Bournonville favored a flexed foot on the *cou-de-pied,* which pointed as it left that position. There are advantages to both types of execution. The pointed foot involves the posterior and anterior muscles of the thigh in a continuous action as the leg is brought from the extended position to a *retiré* position, either in front or in back of the calf. The slow, sustained folding-in of the leg is emphasized, while the unfolding to the extension can be experienced almost as a release of tension. With the flexed foot on the *cou-de-pied,* all the muscles of the calf are involved in a gentle flexion and extension. Mobility of the ankle joint is increased, and this benefits all jumps and strengthens the ankle for *pointe* work.

The question of coordination is important in both versions. With the constantly pointed foot, both legs bend and stretch at the same rate, so that the *demi-plié* of the supporting leg is matched by the arrival of the working leg to the calf; similarly both legs are fully stretched at the same time. When a flexed foot is used, an added coordination problem arises. When leaving the *cou-de-pied,* the foot must be pointed immediately and must not anticipate the flex when it returns to the *cou-de-pied.* Rather, it must come to rest on the *cou-de-pied* in a flexed position precisely at the moment when the supporting leg has reached the full extent of its *demi-plié.* In either version both legs are then in position to start the next unfolding at the same time.

There is some controversy concerning the place of *fondu* in the sequence of *barre* exercises. Some teachers favor the introduction of *fondu* after *rond de jambe par terre,* while others place it between *battement jeté* and *rond de jambe par terre.* If *fondu* is used primarily as a placement exercise, the leg never exceeding an angle of 45 degrees to front and side and 15 degrees to the back, and if it incorporates the Bournonville flexed foot, then it rightfully belongs after *battement jeté*. But, if the height of the extension is being stressed, the pointed foot coming in to the calf, then *fondu* should not be done until after *rond de jambe par terre* has explored and warmed the area of the hip joint. Of course, both versions can be used within a single sequence, beginning with the low *fondu* and gradually increasing the height.

Battement fondu can be done in all positions besides the basic front, side, and back. In *croisé, effacé,* and *écarté,* the arms and upper body assume an active part in the movement, adding an extra coordination problem that must be solved smoothly. The arms describe a full *port de bras* with each *fondu* and arrive at their destination at the moment of full extension. In advanced classes, *demi-* or even *grand rond de jambe en l'air* can be included in the combination, each movement being linked by a *demi-plié.* To wit: *fondu* to the front, *demi-rond de jambe* to the side, *fondu* to the side, *demi-rond de jambe* to the back, *fondu* to the back, *demi-rond de jambe* to the side, two *fondus* to the side; the sequence is then repeated in reverse; and finally the whole exercise is performed with a rise onto *demi-pointe.*

This exercise is a basic preparatory movement for both *adagio* and *allegro.* It is especially valuable in instances when a slow descent from full *pointe* is required, but indeed it prepares for all soft, controlled landings onto one leg. It conditions the body for such a landing and develops the muscles that support a centered placement of the pelvis.

While *battement fondu* is an excellent, thorough warming-up exercise, it also influences and determines the correct execution of many steps in the center. Its importance in developing suppleness in the legs and the hip joint, its use of coordinated movement involving the whole body, and its role in establishing and keeping a secure center make it one of the most useful exercises of the classic *barre.*

A word of caution is necessary at this point: This exercise should not be introduced to beginners since a certain amount of proficiency must be established before a correct and therefore beneficial execution can occur. Beginners, especially young ones, possess neither the coordination nor the control to cope with the problems inherent in *battement fondu.* These problems are better approached in isolation using other less complex exercises such as *battement frappé* for the correct position of the working foot on the *cou-de-pied, rond de jambe par terre* for the rotation of the femoral head in the hip socket, and simple *développé* for the extension of the leg.

Ronds de Jambe par Terre

This exercise is the first rotary movement at the *barre* (at least in the case of beginning students), and it is the most basic form of a smooth continuous rotation of the femoral head in the hip socket. In *rond de jambe par terre* the working leg (toes pointed and never losing contact with the floor) describes a circular motion, its foot being as far away from the supporting leg as the natural length of the limb will allow. *En dehors* the motion proceeds from front to back; *en dedans* it goes from back to front. Each circling is linked to the next one by a passage through first position during which the whole foot regains contact with the floor.

The preparation for *ronds de jambe par terre* is a *dégagé devant* on *demi-plié* and a *demi-rond de jambe* to second position *pointe tendue*, the supporting leg straightening during the half circle. To do the motion *en dehors* the working leg proceeds to the back, then through the first position it extends to the front and immediately begins the next circling. The rotation of the femur is gradual and constant, and the arrival at each point of the circle is turned-out. The thigh should be felt to be uplifted and supported by the inside muscles of the leg, specifically the sartorius and gracilis, especially in the position to the back. For the *rond de jambe en dedans*, when the leg circles from back to front, the heel and the inside of the leg lead the motion in order to insure the constancy of the turn-out.

The exercise is meaningful only if a continuous rotation in the hip socket is experienced. Its turn-out, as always, is controlled at the top of the leg. The degree of turn-out is dependent upon the position of the femoral head within the acetabular cavity and upon the strength of the deep rotators which hold it. A forced turn-out of the feet will not only inhibit the proper development of connecting and protective muscles but will also build an unsuitable musculature, often leading to injury through misalignment. A badly turned-out heel may only be a symptom of an inadequately rotated femur. On the other hand, there is a certain mobility in the ankle joint that allows the foot to slip out of alignment. The ankle and its supporting tendons and muscles are weakened when the foot is allowed too much play. Passage through first position is a critical moment, one when the alignment of foot to leg may be lost. As a useful test for the correct alignment of the whole leg, do the *rond de jambe* with a flexed foot. Here the rotation of the femoral head can be isolated, and the student can then be encouraged to feel the same muscular process as when the foot is pointed.

Another fault to guard against is a foreshortening of the leg during the circling. It usually happens this way: The working leg becomes decidedly shorter than the supporting one, and it cannot regain full contact with the floor during the passage through first position. This fault is not limited to the *ronds de jambe* for, in students with such tendencies, it also seems their habitual mode of executing *battement tendu, jeté,* and even *grand battement.* It inhibits the free rotation of the femoral head, brings into play the gluteus group of muscles (developing them beyond their usefulness or attractiveness), and distorts the placement of the pelvic bowl. This fault is easily corrected once the student becomes aware that it is not necessary to contract the quadriceps voluntarily in order to disengage one leg from the other. These muscles will contract naturally to the degree needed to perform the motion.

This exercise is often taught to beginners with a stop in each of the four positions. Continuous motion is introduced later. *Ronds de jambe par terre* can also be done with the supporting leg on *demi-plié;* the weight of the body is fully on the supporting leg while the pelvis remains level. As the working leg draws into first position, the supporting leg is stretched, allowing the working leg to remain taut throughout the exercise. A *port de bras* with *cambré* generally closes a sequence of *ronds de jambe par terre.* It can be as simple as a forward and backward bending of the body while the feet are in fifth position or as complex as a *grand port de bras* with the working leg extended in the back and the supporting leg in deep *demi-plié,* the *cambré* stretching forward over the supporting leg and extending back while the weight remains on the supporting leg.

Rond de jambe par terre prepares for the correct execution in the center of *pas de basque, soutenu en tournant,* and *pas de bourrée en tournant.* It increases the mobility in the hip socket and builds the control necessary for a sustained turn-out. It is also beneficial to the ankle joint and reinforces the correct foot position first experienced with *battement tendu.*

Battements Frappés

Battement frappé is a sharp low extension of the lower leg while the thigh is held strongly in place. Preparation for it begins, as it does for *fondu,* with a *dégagé* to second position *pointe tendue,* followed by placing the foot on the *cou-de-pied* with a flexed ankle. The first part of the movement is a striking outward, the ball of the foot grazing the floor until the leg is straight, toes fully pointed. The second part of the movement is a return to the *cou-de-pied* position. The dynamics of the *frappé* are sharp and strong, the accent occurring when the leg is straight. The forcefulness is limited to the outward thrust, the lower leg returning smoothly to the *cou-de-pied*.

Frappé can be executed to the front, side, and back, but to beginners it is generally taught only to the side. The thigh is held well turned out and immobile when the action is to the side. When *frappé* is performed to the front or back, it is permissible for the thigh to move a little in the direction of the movement as long as the femur preserves its outward rotation in the hip socket. The thigh establishes the angle of the *frappé*, which should not be above 15 degrees. Its enforced immobility demands that the deep rotators of the hip joint be fully active throughout the exercise.

The flexed foot on the *cou-de-pied* is an important component of the movement. It conditions a quick reflex action in the ankle joint and strengthens that area at the same time. The foot must be aligned to the turn-out of the knee and hip in both the flexed and the stretched positions. Proper alignment eliminates any play in the ankle joint and strengthens not only that joint but also the knee through the interplay of connecting muscles.

Some schools teach *frappé* with a fully pointed foot on the *cou-de-pied*. The flexed foot may not be as pretty as a pointed one, but (as with *fondu)* this reasoning does not justify omitting the flex. When the foot alternately flexes and stretches, the mobility, strength, and speed of response in the ankle joint are greatly increased. Many *allegro* steps rely on a quick, strong reflex in that area for precision and speed. *Frappé* with a flexed foot nurtures these qualities.

Frappé can be beaten, in which case it is called *double* or *battu*. In *frappé battu* to the side, the working foot, from its initial position on the *cou-de-pied*, will bypass the supporting ankle with a slight outward swing, beat the back of the ankle, return to beat the front of the ankle, and strike out to the stretched position in second. To reverse the exercise, the foot beats front, then back, then extends to second position. If *frappé battu* is done *en croix*, the sequence of beatings will be as follows: the foot beats back, front, and opens to the front; then it beats front, back, and opens to the side; then it beats front, back, and opens to the back; and finally it beats back, front, and opens to the side. From this description it can be deduced that if the opening is to the front, the second beating prior to the opening is also to the front; and if the leg is coming from an opening to the front, the first beating must be in front. Execution to the back follows the same rules. To the side the beatings usually alternate, first front–back, then back–front.

Frappé can also be executed with a *demi-plié* on the supporting leg when the working leg is traveling out. This variation increases the potential for *ballon*, especially if the dancer rises on *demi-pointe* as the working leg returns to the *cou-de-pied*. The dynamics are not changed by the introduction of *plié;* the accent still occurs when the leg is in the open position. The return to the *cou-de-pied* is done in a comparatively nonaggressive manner.

It is sometimes useful to contrast the outward thrust of *battement frappé* with the inward accent of *battement raccourci* in the same combination. In this case the *raccourci* will end in front or back of the calf, not in fifth position, as previously described in connection with *battement jeté.* The position of the thigh is slightly higher for *raccourci* than for *frappé,* and a transition needs to be introduced between the types of *battement.* However, once the thigh is in position, it is not allowed to fluctuate in height during the execution of a series of the same kind of *battement.* As a simple example let us consider four *frappés* followed by four *raccourcis,* all to the side. Three of the *frappés* will be done in the manner and to the height described earlier, while the fourth will be executed at an angle of 67 degrees (halfway between 45 and 90 degrees).

The leg is now in position to begin *battement raccourci.* The force previously used in the outward motion is now used to bring the foot in toward the calf. The accent is "in," which implies a slight stop when the leg has arrived at the calf. The foot is fully pointed throughout the motion. The thigh is held firmly at its new height and not allowed to wave up and down. (The four *raccourcis* are executed in this fashion.) After the last *raccourci,* the foot descends from the calf height to the *cou-de-pied* and is in position to begin *battements frappés.* This transition allows the foot to slip down to the ankle while the thigh resumes its angle of 15 degrees and the ankle flexes. This exercise is especially beneficial to the execution of *ballonné* and *ballotté* in center work. The dynamic action both in and out involves primarily the lower leg, strongly supported by a placed, immobile thigh.

Battement frappé develops speed and strength in the leg and ankle. It also helps to isolate the muscular involvement of the deep rotators of the hip joint, which must enforce the outward rotation even while a great deal of activity is happening in the lower working leg.

Ronds de Jambe en l'air

This exercise begins with a straight, outward thrust of the working leg to an angle of 90 degrees in second position. The thigh is held in position while the lower leg describes an oval, the foot coming toward the supporting knee and out again to the stretched position. When the movement is performed *en dehors*, the lower leg sweeps backward, passes the knee, and proceeds forward before opening to second. The *en dedans* motion reverses that process, the leg describing an oval forward, passing the knee, swinging a little backward before opening to second. The oval is only as big as the flexibility of the knee will allow without disturbing the position of the thigh. The thigh itself moves neither up nor down, front nor back. Activity is limited to the lower leg, the immobility of the thigh thus requiring the knee to perform a circular motion. The foot remains fully pointed throughout the action.

Ronds de jambe en l'air can be taught singly with the working leg closing in fifth after each revolution. After *ronds de jambe en dehors* the working leg closes in the back; after *ronds de jambe en dedans* it closes in front (always!). The exercise can also be done in a series: The working thigh remains in second position while three or more revolutions are executed, then the leg closes in the appropriate manner. Each of the circlings must end in the fully stretched position before the next one begins.

For beginners the circling is broken down into two parts: the in motion when the foot touches the supporting knee (back–front for *en dehors*, front–back for *en dedans*) and the out motion when the leg straightens. Holding the thigh in position at 90 degrees is often perceived by beginners as the sole responsibility of the quadriceps. Contraction of that muscle group is easily felt and mistakenly assumed to be a necessary part of working hard. There are numerous muscles in the pelvic areas as well as the legs themselves that cooperate both in the holding and in the moving. The surface muscles, along with the deeper ones, should always be worked in their full length, never by enforcing a harsh contraction which shortens the muscles too much and eventually builds bulk.

Double ronds de jambe are usually done within the same amount of music allowed for a single *rond de jambe*, but the working leg performs two circlings before opening to the stretched position. A good way to improve speed in execution is to open to the stretched position after each circling; that is, to execute a series of single *ronds de jambe* at double time.

The exercise can also begin with a *petit développé devant* on *demi-plié*, followed by *demi-rond de jambe* (supporting leg straightening) to second position. A series of *ronds de jambe en dehors* follows, the last one closing in fifth position back. The exercise is reversed by beginning with a *petit développé derrière* on *demi-plié*, followed with a *demi-rond de jambe* to second position and a series of *ronds de jambe en dedans*, the last one closing in fifth position front. The *petit développé* is done at an angle of 90 degrees, the leg remaining at the same height during its journey to the side.

This combination is a valuable means of experiencing the dynamics of a *fouetté en tournant* before a turn is attempted. In advanced classes, when an actual turn is included in the combination, the *fouetté* may finish in *attitude derrière* after a turn *en dehors* or in *attitude devant* after a turn *en dedans*. The finishing can be with a stretched leg at 90 degrees in second position after either turn.

Besides benefiting the execution of *fouettés*, this exercise helps achieve control in all *adagio* work in the center. It also prepares for *allegro* steps like *ballotté, gargouillade, pas de chat, renversé,* and *saut de basque. Ronds de jambe en l'air* strengthen the whole leg and increase the flexibility of the knee joint.

Développés

Développé is a slow sustained unfolding of one leg in any position to a maximum height. Beginning usually in fifth position, the working leg is lifted into a *retiré* position and, without stopping at the height of the supporting knee, continues to unfold until the leg is straight in the desired direction.

As the working foot is lifted to the *retiré* position, the quadriceps are stretched and the sartorius monitors the turn-out down to the knee. As the leg unfolds, the hamstrings group extends while the quadriceps contract until the knee is taut. Once the leg is fully stretched, the flexors of the hip joint and pelvic area, primarily the iliopsoas, help to maintain the position. The height of the extended leg is determined by the height of the knee prior to the extension: the leg cannot drop below the *retiré* position.

The logistics of *développés* are slightly different depending on the direction of the extension. During *développé devant* the back must remain perfectly straight. Any tendency to curve the pelvis under in order to achieve a greater height must be resisted. The lumbar region of the spine remains aligned to the rest of the vertebral column. This alignment not only strengthens the torso but also allows a real lengthening of the hamstring muscles. In *développé* to the side, the hip on the side of the working leg will inevitably lift when the extension is above a 90-degree angle. The displacement must not be anticipated, however; it is the result of the height of the extension, not a preparatory action preceding it. Beginners should keep the leg at 90 degrees, even if they are very supple. The higher extension requires a strong musculature to cope with the stress to the skeletal alignment, a strength they do not yet possess. To the back the thigh is lifted and, passing through an *attitude*, the leg stretches to the back. The pelvis responds to the height of the leg by tilting forward above the femoral connection of the hip joint. The spine must remain long even as it curves; the most noticeable upward sweep is located in the lower cervical and upper dorsal regions. Abdomen and diaphragm are supportively taut to relieve some of the tension created in the middle back (the lumbar area) by the height of the leg. Shoulders and pelvis remain aligned on the sagittal plane. The pelvic bone, on the side of the supporting leg, is not allowed to collapse on top of the thigh; it remains uplifted and preserves the length of the hip joint ligaments and the supporting muscles of that area.

When the leg is lowered from any position, it should not be foreshortened. The quadriceps must not be allowed to bunch up in the effort to control the lowering of the leg. This fault is particularly prevalent from front and side extensions.

There are as many ways to vary a *développé* combination as there are dance teachers in the world. The most basic form of the exercise is one *développé en croix*, closing in fifth position after each extension. It can also be done omitting closing in fifth after each *développé* and instead linking the extension by a high *raccourci* to the knee. As yet another variation it can be done with a *demi-plié* on the supporting leg. The supporting leg will bend as the working leg leaves the *retiré* position. It will straighten when the working leg returns to fifth or to *retiré*. This exercise is especially useful for male dancers because it strengthens the legs for jumps. Combinations of *demi-* or *grand rond de jambe*, *penché* in *arabesque*, *grand fouetté*, and the use of the nine positions detailed in Chapter 7 with appropriate arms, all help to make this an endlessly variable exercise.

Développés are executed with the aim of transcending one's limitations while adhering to the rules of good posture and placement of the classic technique. They require perfect coordination between limbs and body. They develop control, balance, and flexibility in preparation for all steps requiring aplomb, both for men and women, and they groom the female dancer for supported *adagio* work.

Petits Battements sur le Cou-de-pied

Petit battement is a deceptively simple exercise. The preparation is the same as for *battement frappé:* the working foot opening to second position is placed on the *cou-de-pied*. It is slightly flexed at the ankle; the longitudinal arch wraps around the supporting ankle bone, while the toes graze the floor. The thigh is held in a turned-out position throughout the exercise. The action is all below the knee. The working foot bypasses the supporting one with a slight outward swing gently striking it in back then in front. When the exercise is done on a flat foot the working toes never fully stretch or lose contact with the floor, but when it is executed on *demi-pointe* the flex of the working ankle becomes less pronounced and the toes stretch downward.

This exercise can be done on *demi-plié* as well as on *demi-pointe*. It can be a continuous, even beating, or it can be done with an accented stop either in front or in back of the supporting ankle. The stop itself can be further defined by a short *demi-plié* or a rise to *demi-pointe*. A tiny *développé* to a *pointe tendue* position in any direction can also be included in a combination. To finish a sequence on *demi-pointe*, *battement battu* or *serré* is often used. *Battement battu* beats only in front or in back of the supporting ankle rather than alternating. In front, the lower leg swings in and out, rather like a pendulum, and beats the front of the supporting ankle, the foot being fully pointed. To the back, the action is slightly different. The lower leg swings backward from the knee, the side of the working ankle striking the back of the supporting one. A *port de bras* generally accompanies this version of the exercise, *en dehors* when the foot beats in front and *en dedans* when it beats in the back.

Petit battement par terre is a variation used by the Russian school. In this case the working foot does not leave the floor at all, but slides out just far enough to bypass the supporting heel on its journey from fifth front to fifth back (back and forth). This movement duplicates almost exactly the action which happens in the air during a beaten *allegro* step. The connection between *petit battement* and *petite batterie* is more easily understood by students when illustrated with this form of the exercise.

The influence of *petit battement* is far-reaching. The exercise strengthens the deep rotators of the hip joint by the enforced immobility of the thigh, and it adds to the flexibility of the knee itself by the relatively free-swinging motion of the lower leg. It develops speed and precision for *petite batterie* as well as for high beaten steps like *assemblé volé battu*. Because it enforces a strict control of the thigh, it also is of benefit to the execution of *chaîné* turns. *Pirouettes sur le cou-de-pied* also owe much to the correct placement of the leg during this exercise.

This little exercise is often perceived by students as a rest period between a strenuous *adagio* and an exacting *grand battement*, yet it is as central to the classic technique as the all-important *plié* itself.

Grands Battements

Grand battement is essentially a high kick, but one invoking such classic precepts as the well-turned-out leg, straight back, and pointed foot. Toward the end of the *barre* the whole body is warmed and placed, so that the full extent of force and energy at a dancer's disposal can be used safely. Like many preceding exercises, *grand battement* involves a disengagement of one straight limb, but now the limit of the kick is the dancer's own extension. The kick can be done in any direction, but most frequently is performed *en croix* using a series of two or more in the same direction. Extension upward should be felt to come as much from the hamstrings as from the inevitable contraction of the quadriceps. Yet, again, these should not bunch up in a foreshortening. The tendency to foreshorten the quadriceps is hard to resist in the descent when gravity weighs down the leg. The pull of gravity should be minimally resisted, just enough so that the leg is not dropped into fifth position, the limb being quite taut yet free of unnecessary tension.

When performed to the front, there should be as little displacement as possible in the pelvic area. As with *développé devant*, the lumbar region of the spine must remain straight and long, the abdominals taut in order to support the deep muscles of the spine, and the upper body free of tension. When done to the side, the working hip will shift up at the height of the kick, but the displacement must not be anticipated. Rather, it should come as a response to the kick; the hip returns to the level placement as soon as the descending leg allows. To the back, the pelvis tilts forward at the hip joint (again only in response to the height of the leg), and returns to its original upright position as soon as the leg is low enough to allow it. The immediate return to center from a side displacement as well as from a forward one is essential. It conditions the body to recover from high jumps like *grand jeté* and *grand jeté en tournant* or from a high kick coupled with a jump of one or both legs, such as *pas de papillon, temps de ciseaux,* or *temps de flèche.*

Besides the obvious variations on this theme, such as *grand battement* rising on *demi-pointe* or finishing in a *demi-plié,* or *grand battement jeté* which literally throws the leg in a *grand rond de jambe en l'air* from front to back and vice versa, there are two variations especially worth mentioning. The first is *grand battement développé,* which begins with a high *retiré,* proceeds without a stop to a full, straight extension, and then returns to fifth position. The second is *grand battement enveloppé,* which begins as a regular *grand battement* with a straight knee, but at the height of the kick the knee bends and the leg passes through a *retiré* position before closing in fifth. Yet another valuable alternative is the *grand battement balancé* or *en cloche,* in which the leg swings from front to back, passing through first position. This version usually begins with a preparation to *pointe tendue derrière;* the swings remain even and continuous until the last one is arrested in *arabesque* and held to balance. The inside muscles of the leg (hamstrings, sartorius, and gracilis) lead in the extension to the front and support the leg in the extension to the back. If these muscles are actively involved, it will be easier to preserve the turn-out both at the height of the kick and in the descent and transit through first.

Many of the good habits established through earlier exercises will be tested with *grands battements.* Foremost among them are correct extension of the leg without loss of turn-out, which was experienced with *battements tendu* and *jeté;* and correct pelvic positioning, which was fostered by *fondu* and *développé.* The *battement* must be free to rise and descend; it must be controlled without being coerced, convulsed, or otherwise inhibited by extraneous muscular contractions. These two conditions presuppose a developed flexibility in the hip joint, a comfortable familiarity with the balletic stance, and an ability to regain a square placement on both legs when the working leg returns to fifth position.

Each motion or exercise may be but one stitch making up a tapestry; and yet each stitch must be perfect if the tapestry is to be flawless; each is used individually to create a balanced design.

Chapter 7

Positions

The dancer and the choreographer work within a specific space. In most cases that space is a proscenium stage. On stage the dancer addresses his movement to the audience. Motion is possible in any direction—from wing to wing, upstage to downstage and vice versa, diagonally, and in circles. The dancer has choice not only of direction but of position as well. The dancer who always faces the line of direction instead of the audience would quickly become dull and predictable; if the dancer always faced the audience, the same monotony would be apparent.

Both predicaments can be avoided by giving the body independence from the legs and the line of direction. In classic dance the dancer and choreographer have at their disposal not only the means to relate to the space but also the means to explore all the expressiveness inherent in the human structure by the use of *épaulements* and body positions.

In the classroom the mirror takes the place of the audience. The dancer's attention is always drawn to her own reflection in order to check, adjust, and correct her poses. But the reliance on the mirror must not interfere with *épaulement* and body positions, which add subtle yet important shades to the execution of all steps.

The positions of the body are established both by the relationship of the dancer to her space and by the relationship of the dancer to her own axis. There are nine positions of the body around its axis. We will first examine them in their static form. However, they can also be used while traveling from one spot to another.

The classroom space, or stage, is divided into front, back, and two sides. For clarity, we are numbering the sides and corners from one to eight clockwise, with the front or audience located at number one. Let us now place the dancer in the center of this square, and then describe the positions as performed on the right side.

Three basic positions do not involve any twisting or turning around the axis. They are the *en face* positions to the front, side, and back. Three additional positions make use of the *épaulement* by bringing

Floor Diagram

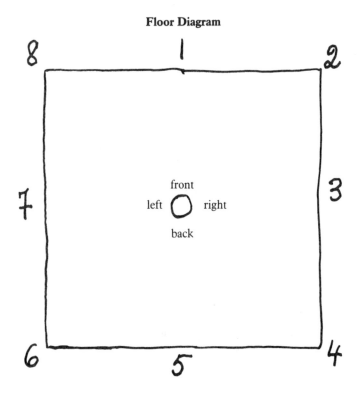

one side of the body forward; the result is a spiraling action around the axis. These positions are: *croisé* (crossed over), *écarté* (separated), and *effacé* (open). These positions can also be qualified as oppositional or complementary. An oppositional pose requires the opposite side of the body to the front leg to be emphasized, as in walking when we step out with the right leg and swing the left arm forward. A complementary pose emphasizes the same side of the body as the front leg. *Croisé* and *effacé* positions can both be complementary and oppositional depending

Positions

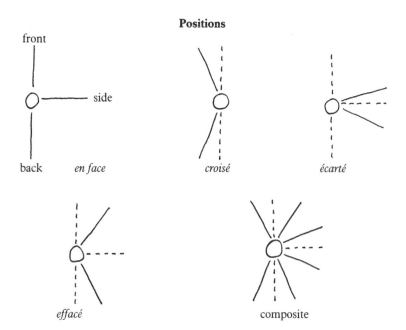

front

side

back   *en face*   *croisé*   *écarté*

effacé   composite

on the arms' position. When a *croisé* or an *effacé* position is complementary, it can be termed "*épaulé*" for clarity; for example: *croisé devant épaulé*.

As can be seen from the illustrations, *croisé* and *effacé* can be executed front and back, while *écarté* qualifies the second position. Each of these positions has a corresponding position of the arms and head.

In Beaumont and Idzikowski's *A Manual of the Theory and Practice of Classical Theatrical Dancing (Cecchetti Method)*, eight directions of the body are illustrated. These are the same as the ones covered here except for *écarté derrière*, which is omitted from the book. In the Cecchetti system, the various positions are achieved by preserving the *en face* alignment and rotating the whole body to face a new direction, be it *croisé*, *effacé*, or *écarté*. Thus the dancer presents a different perspective to the audience from each position. The parts of the body, however, are still aligned on the same plane; there is no rotation about the dancer's own axis; and the femoral heads in the hip socket do not change their basic *en face* position. This manner of executing the positions leaves out a very important facet of motion: mobility of the body. In this instance the dancer experiences only the three basic positions: front, side, and back. To qualify them he creates a new front-in relationship to fixed points outside himself.

The nine positions of the body as described here are not based solely on the acquisition of a new front, but rather take into account other considerations that qualify the position of the body and that prevail no matter where the front happens to be. These considerations are grounded in the actual relationship of the body to its axis. The position of the femur in the hip socket determines whether the movement is to the front or side, whether an *arabesque* is *croisée* or *effacée*. The spiraling action of the back and the position of arms and head further define the position, so that each one is distinctly characteristic and clearly delineated. This system of execution is taught by Cleo Nordi, who, I presume, learned it from Nicolas Legat.

In assuming the *épaulé** positions of the Legat School, the dancer uses his supporting leg as a pivot and rotates the body above that pivot in order to achieve the desired angle or direction. This method of execution encourages the fullest development and flexibility of the rotation in the hip socket. A dancer is able to experience the movement in relation both to some fixed point outside the body and to actual physical changes around his axis. Control and strength of the muscles surrounding the rotating head of the femur in the hip socket are thus increased, and a wide choice of direction in motion is developed. The pivotal-spiraling action, however, requires a well-established turn-out, and is therefore not recommended as a teaching method for beginners. The Cecchetti system familiarizes the student with the possible directions a movement may take. The Legat system refines that knowledge; it is the fine tuning that an artist expects from his instrument.

Each position is illustrated here with a description of a *dégagé* to *pointe tendue*. However, these positions are so basic to the classic technique that every step makes use of them in some way. By understanding these positions in their simplest aspect, the dancer begins to perceive clearly the more complex movements of center work, both *adagio* and *allegro*. (In the exercises that follow, one way to appreciate them better is to actually perform them.)

In *croisé devant* (front), as the foot extends to *pointe tendue*, the pelvis and shoulders face the direction of the opening leg. The supporting leg remains in its original alignment, *en face*. The arms pass through first position and open respectively to the side for the right arm, and above the head for the left arm (fourth position *en haut*). The head is slightly inclined and turned toward the front shoulder (right). The

---

**Epaulé* is a general term used to describe a movement that is not *en face*. It is also used to designate a particular position of the body *(arabesque épaulée)* in which the head is turned toward the front shoulder and the front arm is extended forward.

Croisé Devant

Croisé Epaulé Devant

eyes are focused outward in the same direction. In relationship to the space, the extended leg points toward corner 8; the right arm is in line with corner 2; the left arm's elbow is in line with corner 6; and the head faces side 1 but is inclined toward corner 2.

In *croisé derrière* (back), as the foot extends to *pointe tendue*, the pelvis and shoulders face corner 2. The left arm is above the head; the right arm is in second position (fourth *en haut*). The head is inclined toward the right shoulder, but faces front, as if looking under the arm. Another way of executing this position is with the right arm up and the left open to the side. In this case the head may face corner 2. In *croisé derrière* the angle of the pivot is at its most acute. Stress will be felt from the longitudinal arches, the side of the knee, and the inside of the thigh; but no pronation should occur if the integrity of the alignment is to be preserved.

In relationship to the space, the extended leg points toward corner 6; the arms are on the diagonal line of corners 8 and 4. When the left arm is up, the head is turned and inclined to corner 8; when the right arm is up, the head faces front.

The *effacé* position makes use of a spiraling upward action in the upper back (similar to the spiral achieved by modern dancers, as in some floor exercises of the Graham technique), and it also utilizes the pivoting action above the supporting leg, already experienced in the *croisé* position.

In *effacé devant*, the foot opens to a *dégagé* front. The pelvis and shoulders turn to the direction of the opening leg, while the supporting leg remains in its original *en face* position. The upper torso arches back. The left arm is above the head; the right arm is in second position (fourth *en haut*). The head is turned toward the left arm and inclined toward the back, finishing the upward curve of the upper back. The chest is uplifted. The feeling is one of surrender in the upper body, with the head cradled in the curve of the left arm. This position, like *croisé derrière*, requires a well-established turn-out, since the stress on the supporting leg is quite intense.

In relationship to the space, the leg is extended toward corner 2. The right arm is open toward corner 4; the left elbow is in line with corner 8; both arms and head are on the diagonal line from corners 8 and 4. The head is turned to corner 8 and inclined, together with the upper body, toward corner 6.

In *effacé derrière*, the leg opens to a wide position in the back. The pelvis and shoulders turn to face corner 8. The supporting leg

Croisé Derrière

Croisé Epaulé Derrière

Effacé Devant

Effacé Derrière

Écarté Devant

Écarté Derrière

retains its original placement. The arms are both in second position, but the palms face down and the right arm is a little above its normal shoulder height. The head is turned and lifted toward the right arm, with the focus skimming the hand and directed out. The feeling is of maximum opening of the body, particularly the upper chest, rather like the figurehead on the prow of ancient ships. There is also in this position, as in the previous one, a definite uplift of the upper body, with a corresponding backward tilt of the head.

In relationship to the space, the leg is extended toward corner 4; the body faces corner 8. The arms are on the diagonal line of corners 2 and 6. The head is turned to corner 2 and inclined back toward corner 4.

The right arm may be placed in front of the body, extended in a second *arabesque* position with the palm down. In this case the *effacé* becomes an *épaulé* position; the uplift of the upper body is less pronounced. The feeling here is more straightforward with the focus to the front, or with the face turned to side 1, over the front shoulder.

The *écarté* position is used to qualify the opening to the side (second position). The extended leg is in front or in back of the true second. In both instances the body is on a diagonal line, the legs and arms enhancing the feeling of flattening out as if between two walls.

In *écarté devant*, the leg is in front of the true second. The body and arms follow this new alignment, giving a splayed-out quality to this position. The right arm is above the head; the left is in second position. The head is turned toward the right arm and uplifted, with the chin pointing into the crook of the elbow.

In relationship to the space, the movement is executed on a diagonal line running from the front half of side 3, toward corner 2, to the back half of side 7, toward corner 6. The head is turned to corner 2.

In *écarté derrière*, the extended leg is in back of the true second. More of a pivotal action is experienced in this position than in *écarté devant*. The right arm is above the head; the left one is in second position. The head is turned toward the left arm and inclined slightly down.

In relationship to the space, the movement is executed on a diagonal line running from the back half of side 3, toward corner 4, to the front half of side 7, toward corner 8. The head is turned to corner 8, and the body is slightly inclined in that direction.

Once these positions are understood in their static aspect, they can be applied to *adagio* and to traveled *enchaînements* in center work. Motion is possible in any direction. The space can be traversed in straight lines, diagonals, or circles. Besides being able to choose the direction of motion, the dancer can select among the body positions to qualify the direction. To illustrate this point, let us take a simple *enchaînement* which can be executed entirely *en face;* that is, facing front 1: *glissade, petit jeté, coupé dessous, ballonné, coupé dessous, chassé en avant, coupé dessous, assemblé dessous.*

The right foot, which is behind, slides out for the *glissade.* The right foot again opens to second position for *petit jeté. Coupé* is with the left foot; *ballonné* is with the right foot. A *coupé* with the left leads into *chassé* forward with the left foot in front. *Coupé* with the right foot is followed by *assemblé à la seconde* with the left.

If we introduce some *épaulement,* the exercise will appear as follows: *glissade écarté devant,* right shoulder slightly forward, the direction toward a point between corner 2 and the midpoint of side 3. *Jeté* finishing in *croisé,* right shoulder remains in front, the body turned slightly toward corner 8. *Coupé* keeps the previous alignment. *Ballonné* finishing in *croisé* brings the left shoulder forward, and the body now is turned to corner 2. *Coupé* retains the previous *croisé* position. *Chassé croisé* travels in the direction of corner 2 while the body remains also in *croisé.* *Coupé* keeps the previous alignment. Finally the *assemblé* is in an *écarté derrière* position, the leg opening toward a point between corner 6 and the midpoint of side 7. *Assemblé* will bring the right shoulder forward; the left leg is in the back so that the exercise can be repeated to the other side. We have limited the description to feet and shoulders, but the involvement and placement of the upper body is implied in the terms themselves.

In the classroom, *enchaînements* are given almost always with side 1 as the front. Even in combinations traveling on a diagonal from upstage to downstage corner, the positions are assumed in relation to the mirror as *en face.* For example, in a simple combination like *failli* and *assemblé,* the traveled line is a diagonal from corner 6 to 2 to the right side, but the body positions are in relation to side 1 as front.

The *enchaînement* begins with the right foot in front, right shoulder slightly forward. As the *failli* reaches its height, the position in the air is *effacé*—the left leg opening to a low *arabesque,* the left shoulder coming slightly forward. As the left leg swings into a fourth position front, the left shoulder remains forward, but now the position is *croisé.* As the right leg opens to second position for the *assemblé,* the right shoulder comes forward and the left goes back to achieve the *écarté devant* position. The *assemblé* finishes front. The body is now in its original starting position. And because the head is always turned or inclined toward the front shoulder, a consciousness of the audience is present throughout the entire *enchaînement.*

An instance where the front changes with the progressing of the dancer is found in circular *enchaînements (en manège)*. The dancer in this case faces in turn all four walls of the room. When a change of direction is necessary, she proceeds squarely toward the next wall. Let us take *piqué en dedans* as an example, with a dancer beginning in corner 8. During the preparation the dancer faces side 1, but as soon as the movement begins, her alignment and focus change to face side 3. She continues to step toward side 3 until a change of direction is needed. The change of direction is effected by stepping toward the next side (5), then toward 7. If the *manège* is to continue, the dancer will then face side 1, and so on. In classical variations which finish with a *manège*, very often the dancer, once having reached corner 6, will proceed on a diagonal from corner 6 to end in corner 2.

The size of the *manège* varies with the number of steps executed in each direction. Thus if the dancer did six *piqués* toward each wall, the circle would be moderately large, but if she did only two, the circle would be quite small. (*Piqués en manège* in the classic repertoire are always done by female dancers.)

As can be seen from these brief examples, coupling body positions with traveled directions will yield an almost endless variety of

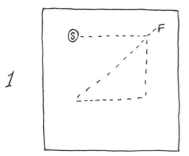

1

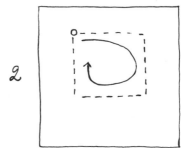

2

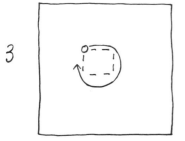

3

Manège

1. A typical *manège* to end a classical variation.
2. A *manège* with six *piqués* to a side.
3. A *manège* with two *piqués* to a side.

patterns. A choreographer can play with the implication of traveling sideways across the space as opposed to a frontal approach, or can discover how the mood of a movement changes when performed in a *croisé* position instead of *effacé*. Although these considerations may seem to belong solely to the choreographic field, the classroom is the place not only where techniques are acquired but also where ideas are born and experimentation can take place.

The basic principles governing the use of the body in space in the classic technique form the language of dance itself, and it is shared by choreographer and dancer alike. Far from inhibiting the creativity of the choreographer, this knowledge will provide a foundation against which to test his own ideas. Moreover, the homogeneity of a *corps de ballet* depends as much on the correctness of the pose as on the purely technical proficiency of the dancers. If learning a step also includes the possible body positions as part of the total concept of that step, then the dancer experiences the language of dance in all its subtlety, and the choreographer can rely on a total familiarity with any given step of his dancers. Thus it is that the dancer becomes an accurate interpreter of choreographic ideas.

Chapter 8

Port de Bras and
Arabesques

No description of dance steps would be complete, nor would a dancer's training be valid, without proper understanding of the role arms play in every motion.

The movement of the legs are divided into (1) paths of travel—when the leg travels from one place to another, and (2) positions—when the leg assumes and holds a specific pose. The arms can be similarly classified. *Port de bras* describes a path or action, and the positions indicate arrival points. As with the legs, there are two principles that underlie the use of arms—aesthetic and physical. The physical refers to the range of motion available to the human frame and the aesthetic, to a pleasing image in terms of the total configuration of the body.

The position of the head and the focus of the eyes play an integral role in the correctness of both the poses and the transitions. The eyes always follow through the direction of the face; if the face is turned toward the audience, the eyes look straight out, if the head is turned or inclined either up or down, the eyes again focus in the same direction. The focus of the eyes is an important component in balance and turns when they help in stabilizing the body. They also help to extend the line by focusing beyond the limits of one's limbs. For example, in an *arabesque* the focus of the eyes does not stop at the hands but extends even beyond the walls of the studio. When a dancer learns to thus project her vision, she has also learned how to include the audience in her motions.

Dégagé to Pointe Tendue Devant Croisé

Landing after a Petit Jeté

The position of the head always refers to the front, the audience, in classical ballet. The aesthetics are based on what will keep the interest of the audience as well as enhance the movement. Therefore, we do not dance with the face always turned to the audience but vary the angles and inclinations. Additionally, the head plays a role in maintaining balance by being positioned over the area that is supported. For example, in a preparation for *rond de jambe par terre*, the head is inclined toward the supporting side, over the leg that is in *demi plié*, in order to keep one's weight stabilized. To incline the head to the other side would endanger balance since the working leg is in an extension and cannot absorb any weight. Similarly, in a *petit jeté*, as the landing occurs the head inclines in the direction of the landing/supporting leg in order to place the body's weight over that side and not jeopardize a safe landing.

The arms perform a number of functions within the technique. Their most obvious role is linking motions of the legs in order to preserve continuity and exhibit an ease of execution. In other words, they mask the effort inherent in movement. Beyond that role they help stabilize the body both in *adagio* and *allegro* by emphasizing the redistribution of weight. They also facilitate turning. The role of arms in *pirouettes* is discussed in the next chapter. We will return to the usage of arms in jumps after examining the positions and some basic *port de bras*.

Although different schools of ballet number positions variously, the positions themselves are basically the same. Cecchetti's numbering system is true to his thorough nature; it is most comprehensive, verging on the pedantic. The French school seems the most logical; the Russian is the simplest to remember but leaves out too many possibilities and usages. We suggest the following numbering system which incorporates features of each school.

Bras bas. Both arms are down and slightly in front of the body, shoulders free of tension, chest open, fingertips about three to four inches apart. Palms face upward. Elbows point to the side.

First position. Both arms are forward in front of the body on the same horizontal plane as the sternum. The curve of the arms is the same as in *bras bas*, but now the palms face the body and the tips of the elbows point outward to the sides. The shoulders remain placed through the motion from *bras bas* to first and the chest remains open. Fingertips again are three to four inches apart.

Bras Bas

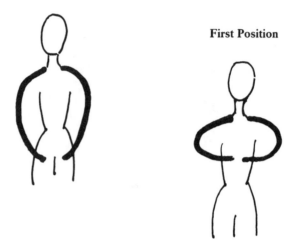

First Position

Second position. Both arms are to the side, the curve is less pronounced than in the preceding positions. The humerus is rotated inward which causes the elbows to be uplifted—the tips of the elbows pointing back. The lower arm is rotated outward which causes the palm of the hand to face forward (toward the front). The extended thumb is in line with the middle finger.

Second Position

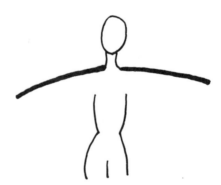

Third Position

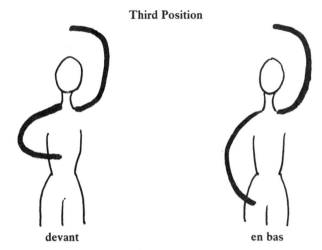

devant   en bas

Third Position. *Devant:* one arm is in first position, one arm is in fifth. *En bas:* one arm is in *bras bas*, one arm is in fifth. This position is generally *épaulé*, the body angled, front shoulder closer to the front. Downstage arm is either in *bras bas* or *devant*, upstage arm is in fifth. The head is turned and slightly inclined toward the front shoulder.

Fourth position. *En bas:* one arm is in *bras bas*, one arm is in second. *Devant:* one arm is in first position, one arm is in second. This is the usual preparation for *pirouettes*. *En haut:* one arm is in fifth position, one arm is in second. As in the previous position, the fourth is also usually performed with *épaulé*. When the upstage arm is in *bras bas*, first, or fifth, the position is *croisé*. When the downstage arm is in *bras bas*, first, or fifth, the position is called *croisé épaulé*. In *croisé* the head can either look over, slightly inclined forward, over the arm in *bras bas* and first position, or it can look out toward the front shoulder which is its position when the arm is in fifth. In *croisé épaulé* the head is turned toward the front shoulder when the arm is in *bras bas* and first position; it can also be inclined toward the back shoulder while still angled to face front. When the arm is in fifth, the head inclines toward the back shoulder and lifts up toward the raised hand.

Fifth position. Both arms are above the head, tips of the elbows face out to preserve the curve of the arms. The wrists finish off the curve of the arms by flexing down. This position is essentially the same as *bras bas* and first in terms of the relationship between upper arm, lower arm,

Fourth Position

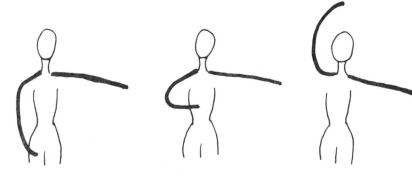

Fourth Position Epaulé en Haut

Fourth Position Epaulé Devant

Fourth Position Epaulé en Bas

Fifth Position

and wrist. In *bras bas* the palm of the hand faces up; in first position it faces the body; now it faces down.

Besides these six positions there are others that involve a rotation of the wrist. These positions include all the *arabesques* and modified positions of the arms in second, third, fourth, and fifth positions. Because of the placement of the hand—palm facing down—and the less pronounced curve of the elbow that elongates the arm, these positions are called *allongé*.

Allongé in second. The wrists turn until the palms face the floor. This position is used in conjunction with *écarté* positioning of the body in movements like *temps liés* and *assemblé volé*. The front arm can be slightly higher than the other. The arms can also be extended beyond the regular second position (slightly behind the body). This position is often used in conjunction with *arabesque*. Additionally, when held below the regular second (Cecchetti's *demi-seconde*), they are used with *soubresaut en arrière*. The head is turned toward the front arm in an *écarté* position except in *croisé* position, like *arabesque croisée*, when the head turns toward the front and inclines slightly.

Allongé in third. From a third position *devant*, the arms extend forward, the palms face the floor. The upper arm (upstage) lowers slightly, the other (downstage) can be slightly raised. The arms should follow the same parallel line. The head can look in the same direction as the direction of the arms and is raised, the eyes focusing over and beyond the higher arm. The head can also be turned toward the lower front arm and slightly tilted toward the front shoulder. This position is used in conjunction with *soubresaut en avant* and *assemblé en avant* as well as the third *arabesque*.

Allongé in fourth. From a fourth position *en haut*, the arms extend. The upper arm lowers slightly; the other arm remains at the same height. Both arms can be extended beyond their positioning in fourth, toward the back, beyond the line of the shoulder. The palms face outward for the upper arm and down for the lower arm. The head is turned toward the front arm, and slightly tilted. It is pertinent to note that this position is similar to the one described earlier for *arabesque ouverte* with *allongé* in second. The difference between them is that now there is a higher arm. In other words, the position originates in fourth *en haut* and not in second where both arms were at the same level. This *allongé* can be performed with the upstage arm higher or with the

Position of Origin

Arabesque Ouverte

Position of Origin

Arabesque Croisée

Arabesque Croisée Epaulé

Position of Origin

downstage arm higher; in both cases the head turns toward the front and tilts slightly toward the downstage shoulder. This position is most often used in conjunction with *arabesques*.

Allongé in fifth. From a fifth position, the arms extend and separate into a wide V, the palms facing outward. The head can either turn toward the front shoulder or look straight forward in the direction the body is facing. The arms can also be taken beyond the line of the shoulders, in which case the upper back arches (the arch is limited to the upper back and does not include the area below the shoulder blades).

Although it is theoretically possible to perform *arabesque* with a variety of arm positions, there are three basic *arabesque* positions which are further qualified as either *ouverte* or *croisée*. All *arabesques* require the palms of the hands to face downward. However, the elbows are not allowed to drop. As in all positions of the arms, the humerus is rotated inward and the lower arm outward, the elbows never fully stretched to preserve the gentle curve or roundness of the arms. The softness of the elbows serves a further function besides the aesthetic. The arms when soft do not reverberate with the impact of landing from a jump and the upper body can remain serene even during the most technically trying motions.

1. *First arabesque ouverte*. Standing on the right leg, the body facing side 3 or corner 2, the left leg is lifted in a *derrière* position. The right arm is extended in front of the body, the left arm held slightly behind the line of the shoulder. The focus of the head is forward toward the front arm, the eyes looking over the hand in line with the middle finger.

First arabesque croisée. Still standing on the right leg the body now faces corner 8. The right arm is extended forward while the left is more markedly behind the line of the shoulder than in the previous *arabesque*. The upper body spirals to bring the dancer's back in view of the audience. The head is turned and slightly tilted toward the front, side 1.

2. *Second arabesque ouverte*. Standing on the right leg, the left is extended *derrière*. The body faces side 3 or corner 2. The right arm is in second position and the left in front of the body. The head is turned toward the front, side 1. This position is also called *arabesque épaulée*. The head can also stay straight looking out toward the front arm.

Second arabesque croisée. Again standing on the right leg, the body faces corner 8 or side 7. The position of the arms is the same as in the previous *arabesque*, although the arm in second position can be

Arabesque with head angled

Arabesque with high arch, head straight

First Arabesque Ouverte

First Arabesque Croisée

slightly back of the shoulder line. Again the head can be angled to the front or look straight out over the front arm.

3. *Third arabesque ouverte.* Standing on the right leg, the body faces side 3 or corner 2. Both arms are extended forward in third position *allongé*, the upstage arm is higher. The head can be turned toward the front and slightly tilted toward the back shoulder or look straight out over the arms.

Third arabesque croisée. Standing again on the right leg, the body now faces corner 8. The upstage arm is higher, with the arm extended in third *allongé*. The head can be turned toward the front and slightly tilted toward the front shoulder or look straight out in the direction of the arms.

No discussion of the arms would be complete without mentioning the hands. A classical hand is softly rounded, fingers curling downward. The thumb extends in a straight line from the wrist across the palm, but not pressing toward the palm. The index and ring fingers are on the same plane, while the second finger falls a little below them and the little finger rises slightly above. There should be no break in the knuckles nor strain in the first phalange of the thumb. This configuration is often seen in Renaissance paintings.

Hands respond to motion by a subtle flexion of the wrist and a straightening of the fingers as the arm travels from one position to another. The naturalness of this response can be greatly enhanced if the dancer thinks of displacing air as the arm moves. This feeling can be experienced more concretely if done under water; the water's weight provides just the right amount of resistance to vividly illustrate what the action should feel like. The dancer can then transpose the feeling from the swimming pool to the studio.

Theoretically, the arms can move from any position to another; however, there are certain rules governing these transitions. All motions have their foundation in the two basic *port de bras: en dehors,* which begins in *bras bas* and passes through first to fifth, opens to second and returns to *bras bas*; and *en dedans,* which begins in *bras bas,* rises to second then fifth, passes through first, and returns to *bras bas*. Besides these two paths, the most commonly used *port de bras* is the one from *bras bas* to first, opening out to second. This is the motion that begins most exercises at the *barre* and in the center. As in all conventions, this opening and placing of the arms is based on specific needs—the necessity to develop the proper musculature and ensure the desired placement or carriage of the upper body. The action of passing through first position to open to second is used to accompany many steps both in

Second Arabesque Croisée

Third Arabesque Croisée

the *adagio* and the *allegro* vocabulary. Additionally, maintaining or holding the arm in second position during *barre* exercises engages the musculature of the back and the front of the torso. Although there is no visible motion when the arm is held in second, by maintaining the position the dancer is developing strong supportive muscles in the upper torso. The pectoralis major, trapezius and deltoids are some of the muscles that can be felt during this action; these muscles and the many others which support arm movement are active from the first moment class begins. Through their development the necessary uplift and opening of the chest become an integral part of the dancer's stance.

The pathways arms take to move from one position to another are as determined as the positions themselves. The shape of the arms is not altered when they rise from *bras bas* to fifth. The roundness is preserved throughout; the wrist remains aligned so that the dancer can look down into the palm of the hand when the arms are down and look up into it when the arms are in fifth. While passing through first position the palms face the body. When opening to second from first position, the motion is felt to originate at the back of the hands, pushing outward; the wrists straighten slightly as the motion begins. The gesture is broad and generous. When the arms return to *bras bas* from second, the movement again begins with the hands; from their forward facing position they turn until the palms face the floor, the wrists flexing slightly downward and the fingers straightening as the arm begins to descend. As the arm nears *bras bas* position, the wrists return to their forward flex position.

In order to complete a *port de bras* from fifth position, the arms open without changing their shape and descend to second. As they near second they turn to assume the position; the palms turn to their forward facing position and the humerus rotates inward to assume the correct second position stance. If the arms are to proceed to *bras bas*, they then turn again as described above. The second position is the place where the transition occurs.

The action is a little different with *port de bras en dedans*. In this case the arms remain in the same alignment as they travel from *bras bas* through second to fifth; in other words, the palms face downward as the arms rise and pass through second, turning to assume the correct fifth position as they arrive in fifth. If the *port de bras* proceeds through first to *bras bas*, the arms maintain their shape just as they did in the reverse direction.

The arms can move independently of one another in any direction, as well as extend to form the *allongé* shapes described earlier.

Thus, while the right arm may be describing a full *port de bras en dehors*, the left arm could open to second position and remain there or could proceed from second to fifth to join the first arm. The head and eyes follow the movements of the arms, with the focus usually toward the front arm.

The arms can combine an *en dehors* with an *en dedans* motion in a variety of ways, so long as they coordinate harmoniously and conform to the shape of the specific positions. In all positions the rotation of the humerus and the uplift and softness of the elbows give the classical arm its rounded quality.

Different schools have conceived a variety of set *ports de bras* which are taught to the students. We have eschewed describing and categorizing each individual possibility in the belief that if one is guided by principles, then the full range of arm motions will be guided by both scientifically and artistically sound concepts. Certain rules, however, need to be observed.

1. The first *port de bras* taught to beginning students is the *en dehors* one—from *bras bas* to second or fifth, it emphasizes the passage through first position as well as the opening to second after the fifth position.

2. At the completion of a *pirouette* the arms open outward, whether the arms were held in first or in fifth during the turn. The most basic position used at the completion of a *pirouette* is the *offrande* position—palms up, arms extended outward and slightly forward below the regular second position. (This subject is discussed in more detail in the chapter on *pirouettes*.)

3. In most jumps the arms travel from a second position to *bras bas* during the preparation *(glissade* or *failli* or *pas de bourrée couru)*, then rise to first position as the body lifts off the floor, then assume whatever position is necessary—*seconde allongée* for *assemblé volé* or fifth position for *saut de basque en tournant* and *grand jeté en tournant*. This action serves to engage the torso in an uplift and gathers the impetus toward the center of the body, making the mass that is to be propelled upward more compact and thus easier to manage.

Finally, one specific *port de bras* needs to be mentioned. It originates in the circular *port de bras* which takes the body forward, then side and back, to return to an upright position, with the accompanying arm and head motions. The *grand port de bras* is executed in a deep fourth position (lunge) with the weight on the front leg in *plié*

B

A

C

E

D

Grand Port de Bras

throughout the motion. In its elementary circling it begins with arms in fourth position (left leg in front in *plié*, right arm up in fifth, left arm in second). Then the body bends forward over the supporting leg, the arms remaining in place. The body then circles to the side (toward the arm in fifth) as the uplifted arm opens to second and the other arm sweeps through first position to fifth. The head turns to look down and sideways toward the arm that is opening to second; the body proceeds toward the back, the left arm is now in fifth and the right in second position. The head turns until it is angled straight back, looking toward the arm in fifth. As the body regains an upright position, the arms again change so that the original arm in fifth returns to fifth directly from second and the other arm returns to second; the head turns toward the left arm that is traveling to second. The ending position is the same as the beginning one.

In the advanced version the movement begins in the same manner as in the preceding movement but at the moment when the body moves toward the *cambré* back position it spirals, right shoulder moving back, left shoulder coming forward, the head tilting backward behind the left arm which is now in fifth, the right arm in second. There is a momentary pause in that position. Then the movement continues until the right arm is again in fifth and the left in second, as at the beginning of the motion. This *port de bras* is traditionally used as a preparation for *pirouettes en attitude* and was a staple in the classes of both Olga Preobrajenskaya and Cleo Nordi.

As the dancer gains in technical proficiency, the arms become more expressive and move with ever increasing fluidity through the various positions. It must be emphasized that the expressiveness of the arms depends not only on their correct positioning but also on the coordination between the arms and the head. Generally the head turns and tilts toward the front arm thus presenting to the audience either a full or a three-quarter view of the face. Despite the apparent complexity, these choices all originate with the most generous and straightforward of motions—the first *port de bras* executed at the *barre*, in which the head slightly tilts toward the *barre* as the arm lifts from *bras bas* to first, then turns, accompanying the motion of the arm as it opens to second.

The carriage of the upper body and the placement of arms and head need to be developed with the same care and attention to detail as the leg movements if qualities of coordination, grace and fluidity are to be fostered or, indeed, if the dancer aspires to a classical style.

Chapter 9

Weight Transference
and Jumps

All his life man strives, often only unconsciously, for balance. Balance is necessary on both the physical and the psychic levels. Our intake of food should balance our energy output. Rest or sleep balances the active waking hours. Gratification of desires and goals has to balance disappointment and pain. We talk of a balanced person as one who is coping with the demands of daily life in a positive manner. Balance is also exemplified by a juggler who, having launched several objects in the air, has to keep the rhythm between these objects constant, adjusting instantly to any deviation from the desired pattern. The dancer in her craft is also a juggler; her own muscles and bones are the objects she manipulates.

The pact with gravity, mentioned earlier, involves a constantly shifting adjustment of mass in relation to one's center and line of gravity. The farther the mass is from the center and axis, the more difficult the achievement of equilibrium becomes. Before proceeding we should qualify the three terms: center of gravity, line of gravity, and axis.

One's *center of gravity* is the midpoint of the body's total weight—55 percent of total standing height in women, 56 percent in men. In other words, the center of gravity is "that point in the body in which all parts balance each other" (Wells and Luttgens, *Kinesiology*, p. 20). Consider a dancer standing in fifth position. Her center of gravity will be found in the pelvic area in front of her sacrum. When the dancer rises to full point, the center moves upward to just below the sternum. When the dancer bends the knees or tilts the body, the center descends to just above the pubis. A dancer learns how to manipulate the center for specific needs by applying pressures and restraints on muscles; in this way she counterbalances movements performed outside the line of gravity. A dancer with a constantly low center of gravity appears heavy and earthbound. The ethereal quality, so admired in classic dance, relies on the center's being located high under the sternum, only occasionally descending below the sacrum.

The *line of gravity* is an imaginary vertical line which passes at a right angle through the center of gravity. Again consider a dancer standing in fifth position. The line of gravity runs through the top of the head, down the center of the body, and ends over the feet; the weight is borne equally by the longitudinal arches. When the dancer assumes the second position, the line of gravity falls equidistantly between the two feet. But when the dancer is in *arabesque,* the line of gravity falls only through the pelvic area and the supporting leg, while the thorax and head move off the line.

The *axis,* our third term, is a line running through the torso. It duplicates the line of gravity when the whole body is vertical, but when the dancer's upper body moves off the line of gravity, the concept of the axis enables him to continue to relate the mass to the center and use the line of gravity as a reference point.

Center of Gravity, Line of Gravity, and Axis

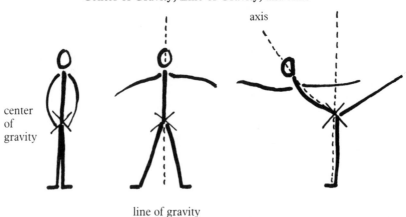

line of gravity

At all times the dancer adjusts his weight around the axis and utilizes the center of gravity as a point of concentrated power from which radiates the energy apparent in all motion. In this discussion we use these concepts where they apply; but when the problems of weight transference are considered, the energy inherent in motion must be our first concern. Keep in mind the general principles of center and line of gravity and their axes. Now let us turn to the comprehensive matter of energy flow, a term we use to define lines of motivation and channels of impulse.

Energy flow determines the attack invested in any movement. The feeling tone of movement depends on the quality of the attack. Thus the energy flow in *adagio* is slow and sustained, rather like a deep river, powerfully yet imperceptibly flowing between its banks. In *petit allegro* the energy flow comes in bursts like the brilliant explosion of fireworks. In *grand allegro* the two qualities are combined into a powerful surge of energy, rather like surf breaking on the beach. Fundamentally, we are dealing with two thrusts or patterns of energy. One is directed outward to produce motion; the second is directed inward toward the center of gravity to maintain balance. Even in so-called static positions there is an energy flow that operates to preserve the status quo.

Energy is directed inward, down from the ribs and up from the lower abdomen. Where the two energies meet can be designated as the center. Feeling the down-in and the up-in helps to keep the shoulders down and the pelvis properly placed, precluding an anteroposterior tilt forward or backward. Yet, as important as these considerations are, another benefit supersedes them. To imagine these open channels of energy enables us to draw on the hidden power of our deep muscles. In the back the energy flows down from the shoulders into and beyond the buttocks, and upward through the spine into the head. The upward energy flow complements the uplift of the waistline and helps keep the structure close to the axis.

Energy is directed outward through the legs and arms. Motion need not stop at the fingertips; rather, it is felt to continue through space. This extension of energy beyond the boundaries of the body gives fluidity to the arms and power to the legs.

We are stressing the idea of energy flow because dance is motion. There is no time when the body is totally static. Even in a prolonged balance, the body is yet in transition from one point of precarious equilibrium to another. These transitions are accomplished by controlling the distribution of weight. The total weight can be involved in an action, or part of it can be held back in order to make a smooth change of direction.

Weight and energy are intimately bound in the execution of all movements. From the first lesson, ballet technique conditions the body to respond effectively, with minimal displacement, to the constant shift of weight. The ability to transfer weight efficiently marks the difference between a tense, jerky execution and a flowing, controlled one. These differences in execution are the result of numerous imperceptible adjustments, and although they are not consciously monitored in advanced dancers, they are nevertheless worthy of analysis.

The energy flows described earlier are present in all motion, but it is in *allegro*, where the weight shifts in the air, that weight transference plays a major role. Let us examine jumps in terms of energy flowing along, around, and beyond one's line, center, and axis.

There are only four ways in which a jump can be executed:

1. From two feet to two.
2. From two feet to one.
3. From one foot to one.
4. From one foot to two.

There is no weight transference in jumps of the first category. Since the push-off is totally vertical, weight is equal on all sides of the body and on the feet; these jumps precondition the dancer to feel the verticality in all jumps.

In the second category, jumps from two feet to one, the push-off is from both feet, but weight is transferred to one leg either at the height of the jump or just before the moment of landing. Although the body is supported by one leg only, the total weight of the body is not allowed to be borne entirely by the leg. Much of it is absorbed by the pelvis. The *plié* of the supporting leg, at the moment of landing, acts rather like the contracting coils of a pogo stick, minimizing the stress of landing but also coiling up for the next jump. Whether the torso is forward of the line of gravity, as in a landing in *arabesque*, or on it, as in a landing on the *cou-de-pied*, the pelvis is always centered. This means that the line of gravity passes through the center of the pelvis; the weight remains close to the axis, which enables the body to recover quickly or change direction without energy loss or time-consuming adjustments.

The weight-absorbing quality of the pelvic area lends lightness to jumps in our third category, from one foot to one foot. The strength of the supporting leg alone would not be sufficient to lift the body off the floor. It is only through the cooperation of the pelvis, which does not allow the total weight of the body to descend onto the foot, that the leg can act as a springboard and propel the body upward. When this type of jump is done from one foot to the other, as in *grand jeté*, the benefits of correct weight transfer in the air are maximized. Three stages of action occur in all jumps from one foot to the other. Weight is on the supporting side to allow a strong, unhindered opening of the working leg; the weight is then transferred to the center to allow the supporting leg to push off effectively; and finally the weight is carried on to the working leg for a safe and balanced landing.

In the fourth category, jumping from one leg to two, the jump begins on one leg, as it does in the jump from one foot to one foot. The same principles apply in the push-off here, and for the landing we can re-apply the centeredness of weight distribution of jumps from two feet to two. The landing is evenly onto both feet.

The determining factor in categorizing jumps is whether the push-off from the floor is performed with the weight equally divided between the two feet, or whether the push-off comes mainly from one foot. The landing follows the same guidelines. Here, in more detail, are some jumps characteristic of each category.

All jumps derived from *soubresaut* come under the first category, jumps from two feet to two. The weight is evenly distributed between the two feet, the push-off is vertical, and the landing is perfectly centered. In *changement* the legs open to the side (only enough to bypass each other) at the height of the jump. The correct execution of *changement* prepares the student for the correct execution of all even-numbered *entrechats*, as well as for other beaten steps. In *echappé*, whether into second or fourth position, the line of gravity falls between the two feet, and the weight is equal for the push-off and the landing. In *retiré sauté* the push-off is again from both feet; while in the air one leg does a quick *retiré passé* and straightens in time for the landing, which again is equally on both feet.

The *ballon*,* so important in jumping, is first experienced in these simple jumps from both feet. The verticality of the push-off determines to a great extent the height of the jump. The verticality of the landing teaches a balanced weight distribution which safeguards ankles and knees from injury.

The energy flow in these jumps prepares the dancer for more complex moves. One's upper body is placed compactly around its axis while the legs thrust against the floor. The verticality mentioned above depends on the ability of the dancer to keep the energy flowing into the center and enforces the connection between the upper body and the pelvis.

---

*Ballon is a child's play ball. The name describes graphically the quality that should be part of any jump. Monsieur Jean Balon (1676–1739) was noted for the lightness of his jump. Some authorities believe that the term was derived from the dancer's name.

Jumps from two feet to one have to be divided into two subgroups: (1) those that end on one leg and (2) those that end in a delayed fifth or fourth position.

The first subgroup comprises all the uneven-numbered *entrechats (trois, cinq, sept)*, as well as all *sissonnes ouvertes* and their derivatives. The push-off, in these cases, is from both feet. The weight is equally divided and the thrust upward is absolutely vertical. (More pressure from one foot than the other will throw the body off the line of gravity.) The legs remain together until the height of the jump is reached. Most beats are done on the descent and not during the initial upward thrust. A slight shift of weight occurs as the supporting leg touches the floor at the completion of the jump.

With *entrechats* one leg finishes on the *cou-de-pied*, back or front. With *sissonnes ouvertes* the shift of weight is more pronounced to counterbalance the pull of the extended leg, as well as to place the pelvis in a favorable position for a good extension. In *devant* and *á la seconde* positions the pelvis remains upright and the upper body counterbalances the weight of the working leg by leaning away from it, thus shifting off the line of gravity. In *arabesque* the pelvis tilts forward and the upper body is in front of the line of gravity.

In all positions, energies that preserve equilibrium are equally active on both sides of the body; the weight of the body comes down into the pelvis equally on both sides, and only then is weight channeled into the supporting leg. Body-mass is upheld around the axis; thus even while the upper body shifts off the line of gravity it preserves its verticality, and weight is not *felt* to be transferred entirely onto the working leg.

The second subgroup of jumps from two feet to one includes all *sissonnes fermées* and steps like *failli* and *temps de poisson* which finish either with a delayed closing into fifth position or a *tombé* into fourth position. In these cases the impact of the landing is on one foot, but the weight shifts quickly to both feet in response to the second leg's coming down into fifth or fourth position. The upper body, which was off the line of gravity at the moment of landing, returns quickly to its vertical position. The pelvis, which was tilted forward, returns to its central position. At that point weight is again even between the two feet. (This description applies to landings into *arabesque;* when the *sissonne* ends in an extension to the front or to the side, the only displacement is in the upper body.)

The return to center, even for an instant, allows a quick transition from one jump into the next. It ensures both a safe centered landing and a vertical push-off for the next jump. And as in the previous group, the upper body, by leaning over the supporting leg, adds color and softness to the transitions.

Jumps in this subgroup (ending in delayed fourth or fifth position) begin in the same way as those in the previous subgroup (ending on one foot). The push-off is from both feet; the legs are held close together until the apex of the jump has been reached. During the descent the legs separate, the working leg extending into the open position, *arabesque, à la seconde,* or *devant.* As the legs separate, the body prepares for the landing by leaning slightly in the direction of the supporting leg (the leg which will first touch the floor).

The majority of *allegro* steps come under the third main category of jumps: those from one foot to one foot. It is sometimes difficult to determine when a jump actually begins since most steps start in a closed position. What happens in the split second between the closed position and the actual push-off from the floor is a matter worth brief notice. When I was twelve, my teacher at the Paris Opera asked me how a *glissade* begins; I answered, "With a *dégagé*." According to her, my answer was wrong. "It starts in fifth position," she said, and sent me out of the classroom for being stupid. The classification we have undertaken would not be possible if she were totally right. For although the point of departure may be fifth position, the actual push-off in this case is from one leg.

There are three subgroups in this category: (1) traveled jumps from one foot to the other, (2) nontraveled jumps from one foot to the other, (3) jumps from one foot to the same foot. Although *glissade* is not strictly a jump, it will do quite well to illustrate the three stages of action involved in jumps from one foot to the other.

The movement begins with a *dégagé* to the side. As the working leg opens from fifth position, weight is transferred from both feet to the supporting side; the extended leg bears no weight. As the supporting leg straightens for the push-off, weight is transferred to center. At that moment both feet are just off the ground and fully stretched. As the working leg touches ground, weight is transferred onto it. The other leg then closes into fifth position, at which point weight again is on both feet.

This series of actions occurs in high jumps from one foot to the other, just as it occurs in a *glissade.* The difference is in the height and therefore in the amount of energy invested in the movement. In a *grand jeté* the weight transfer is more dramatic since it involves both a higher extension and a higher jump. At the beginning of the jump, weight is on the supporting leg, which is in *plié*. The other leg brushes through first position into a *grand battement devant*. As it reaches the height of the kick, weight is transferred forward to center; this allows the supporting leg freedom to kick back and propel the body upward. At the height of the jump, both legs are as close to a split as possible, and the weight is equally distributed throughout the pelvis and the upper body. The propulsion from the floor is not totally vertical since *grand jeté* must travel forward as well as up. As the descent begins, weight is taken forward, over the front leg, in order that the landing may be a safe and balanced one.

Glissade

Grand Jeté

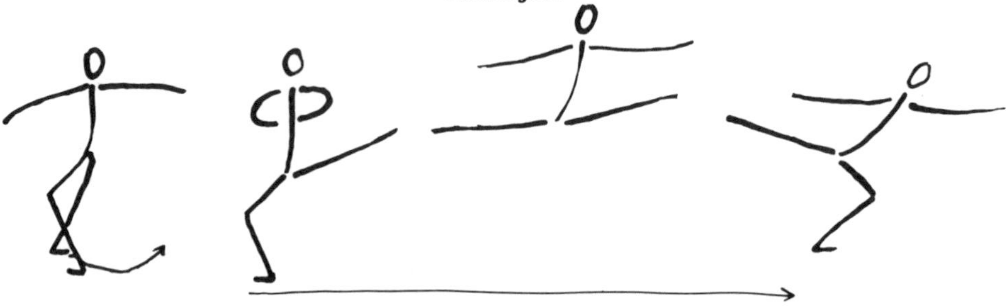

Failure to adjust the weight at each successive stage will affect the height, gracefulness, and safety of the jump. If, at the beginning of the jump, the weight is not on the supporting side, the potential height of the kick will be inhibited. If the weight is not transferred toward the kicking leg before the supporting leg pushes off, the jump will not reach its full potential height, for the supporting leg will be burdened by too much weight from the body. If the weight is not transferred forward over the landing leg, this last stage of the jump will be off-balance, causing stress to the knee and foot. The leg in *arabesque* will lose height and the whole effect will be jerky and somewhat aborted, as well as extremely unsafe.

Most people make these adjustments unconsciously, yet a student who is not jumping as high as he would wish would do well to examine the effectiveness of his weight transference and to determine whether in fact he is in some way working against himself. He may be burdening the pushing-off side with too much weight, or he may be failing to adjust his weight in the air for a good landing. (The arms complement the soaring effect and should not convey any effort or stress.) *Grand jeté* is a traveled jump. The propulsion is up and forward. It can be likened to a long throw which a football player might use to send the ball over the heads of other players and cause it to land at the other end of the field.

In his discussion of *grand jeté*, Dr. Laws (*The Physics of Dance*, p. 36) contends that for maximum push-off the turn-out must be sacrificed:

> Consider two extremes. In the first case the *glissade* preceding the *grand jeté* is performed *en face*, moving directly to the left, with complete turn-out, so that the right foot is pointed directly right as the push off for the *grand jeté* to the left occurs. In the other extreme, the body is turned toward the direction of motion and turn-out is sacrificed, so that the *glissade* becomes a running step to the left, with both feet pointed to the left, in the direction of motion.

In order to make his point, Dr. Laws disregards the precepts of the technique. Most big jumps are taken from a frontal approach, with a few exceptions when the position in the air requires a second position type of splay-out like a *grand jeté a la seconde*. The *glissade* preceding a *grand jeté* travelling to the corner should be executed through a first position into a fourth with the body facing the line of travel (please see the discussion on turn-out in Chapter 3, Posture and Placement). The dancer travelling on a diagonal toward a downstage corner frontally may appear to be slightly turned in from the vantage point of the audience, but is definitely turned out in terms of his own alignment.

The second subgroup comprises nontraveled jumps from one foot to one, among them the *petit jeté*. Although the same series of transfers happens in *petit jeté* as in *grand jeté*, the former ones are not so dramatic. This is so because the supporting leg, instead of thrusting up and along, pushes the body in a strictly vertical direction. After the push-off it bends to finish on the *cou-de-pied* or a *raccourci* position (in front or in back of the calf). The jump finishes on the leg which originally made the extension. This jump is done by substituting one leg for the other on the same spot.

Petit Jeté

and · · · · one · · · · and

The third subgroup in this category includes a wide variety of jumps from one foot onto the same foot. Among these, *temps levé* is the most representative. It is a single or repeated hop on one leg in almost any position: on the *cou-de-pied*, *devant*, *à la seconde*, in *arabesque*, and so on. In all of them the weight is over the supporting leg at the moment of landing and shifts to center as the supporting leg pushes off, to return to the supporting side when landing.

Our fourth and last main category is of jumps which begin on one foot and end on both. The weight transference governing the push-off in the previous category applies in this case also; but as the descent begins, both legs come together in anticipation of the landing, which is evenly on both feet.

Assemblé and *brisé* are the only jumps that truly qualify for this category. The correct execution of the *assemblé*, which is one of the first jumps taught to beginners, conditions both body and mind for the complex components of the numerous jumps in our third main category (from one foot to one foot).

As in *petit jeté*, the push-off for *assemblé* is perfectly vertical, but in the air the leg that opened into the extension comes back to join the supporting leg for an equal landing on both feet. The *assemblé* is done in place except in the case of *assemblé volé*, which travels in the air usually in an *écarté* position. In this instance the propulsion into the air is at an angle, as in *grand jeté*.

Brisé is a low traveling jump, with the added dimension of being beaten. Since a high jump is not desired, the weight of the body need not shift but is kept on the side of the extended leg throughout, with a pronounced tilt of the upper body in the same direction. This stance enables the supporting leg to push off, join the extended leg, beating front-back or back-front, and remain closed for the landing. When executed in quick succession, *brisés* create the feeling that the supporting leg is forever trying to catch up with the extended leg.

The difference between a *brisé* and a *grand jeté* implies a broad principle: the higher the jump, the more vertical the push-off must be. Again consider our football player as an illustration of this point. The angle of his throw will in part determine both the maximum height of the ball and the length it will travel. The closer the throw is to a vertical line the less distance will be covered. If the thrust is completely vertical and there are no outside forces at work, the ball will not travel horizontally. It will simply go straight up and come straight down.

Similarly, a dancer controls the path of his body in space by the angle of the push-off. The position of the body in relation to the push-off, the weight transfer in the air for the type of landing required by the particular jump, and finally the amount of energy invested in the jump, all combine to determine the trajectory.

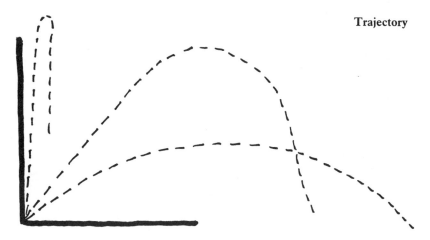

Trajectory

Lightness, quickness, and precision of execution depend on the ability of the dancer to manipulate his weight in relation to his axis. The body is always centered at the outset of a jump; this permits maximum effectiveness. Whether the movement is harsh and thrusting or soft and gliding, the relationship of the parts to the whole must be balanced. The legs, though they are the chief executors, must have the cooperation of the rest of the body; the energy flow through the body affects the

potential energy level and the direction of the thrust of a jump. At this
point the concepts of energy flowing into the center to support the action
and of energy flowing out through the legs to execute the action become
a precondition for motion.

Tours en l'air utilize the same energies with the addition of a
spin around the line of gravity. Simple *tours en l'air* are nothing more
than turned *changements,* and they follow the guidelines governing
jumps of the first category. The weight at the moment of the push-off is
equally divided between the two sides of the body and the two feet. The
thrust upward is absolutely vertical; more pressure on the floor from one
foot than from the other will throw the body off its line of gravity. A tilt
in the upper body or in the pelvic area will have the same detrimental
effect. While a nonvertical push-off may be merely inefficient in the case
of a *changement,* it is courting disaster in the case of a *tour en l'air* because
a clean revolution on the axis thus becomes impossible.

Additional force for the spin comes from the arm's exerting
pressure on the shoulder. The arm's initial outward energy flow must be
reversed and the energy directed back into the shoulder to force it
around. The upper body and pelvis must act as one unit: the whole body
rotates on its axis, perfectly aligned on all planes.

A simple *tour en l'air* begins in fifth position. When performed
to the right, the right leg is in front, the right arm is in first position, and
the left arm is in second. At the moment of the push-off, the right arm
opens slightly to the side, just far enough to engage the shoulder in the
motion. Both arms then come together in first position, at which time
the spin has already begun. The head (as it does in all turns) stays
behind during the first quarter turn, perfectly aligned (the chin neither
droops nor thrusts upward); then it flicks around to the right shoulder,
so that it faces front before the body has completed the revolution.
Simultaneously, while still in the air, the legs do a *changement* so that the
tour ends with the right leg in the back, weight equal on both sides. The
inexperienced dancer must carry his weight in front, when first
attempting a *tour en l'air.* The total verticality of this jump will develop
in time.

If the *tour* is to finish on one foot—*cou-de-pied, arabesque,* and
so on—the principles applied to jumps in our second main category
govern its execution. It is important not to anticipate the final position
on one leg but to wait until the descent has begun before effecting the
transfer. This technique ensures the verticality of the landing.

Many steps in their more complex aspects involve a turn in the air, such as *saut de basque en tournant* and *assemblé en tournant*, both of which are easily performed by female dancers. A great deal of force in both is generated by the kicking leg so that by the time the body is at the height of the jump, half a turn has already been accomplished. For example, an *assemblé en tournant* will be performed in the following way: After the preparation, which is usually a running step *(pas de bourrée couru, glissade,* or *chassé)*, one leg brushes through and kicks to the front as the push-off occurs and the body revolves halfway. As the legs come together at the height of the jump, the turn is completed. The action is the same for a *saut de basque en tournant*; however, at the height of the jump, the leg that executed the push-off comes to a retiré position and remains there as the landing occurs on the other leg. If two turns are to be executed, they are done in the position achieved at the height of the jump, tight fifth position for *assemblé* or *retiré* for *saut de basque*. The action of the arms is an important aspect of the movements. From a second position during the running preparation, they come down to *bras bas,* rise to first as the leg kicks and continue to fifth position where they remain until the conclusion of the jump. Generally the arms open to second position after the landing has occurred. Of course, there may be choreographic divergence from the academic rule; however, it is a mistake to bring the arms from fifth to first *(port de bras en dedans)* as it breaks the outward flow of the motion.

Vaganova states that in *allegro* "the whole wisdom of classical dancing is revealed" *(Basic Principles of Classical Ballet,* p. 12). Weight transference is an inescapable aspect of such motion. From the first moment at the *barre,* when the dancer disengages one leg and stands, however fleetingly, on the other, a transfer of weight is experienced. Unfamiliar motion is monitored; the body quickly internalizes the mechanics to adapt to the problems involved. Consider how fast our minds respond to a flight of stairs that are shallower or steeper than we are accustomed to climbing. The first step may be a jolt, but by the third or fourth we have gauged the distance, computed the information in the brain, and are sending the correct message to the bones. Our stride is lengthened or shortened to navigate the steps without stumbling. Finally the ultimate transcendence of weight transference may be achieved.

A dancer runs, projecting his weight forward for impetus, soars straddling the line of gravity, revolves on his axis, seemingly arresting the motion in mid-air, and lands compactly gathered around his center of gravity to rebound in another leap. One moment his energy is flowing outward, cleaving passages through space, then it spirals into inner channels to gather power for the next bound. His bones and muscles are so finely tuned and so responsive to the commands from the brain that action no longer need be consciously monitored. The wisdom of his training has been translated into freedom.

Chapter 10

Principles of Turning

There is magic in spinning. Our ancestors knew it and invoked their gods with that motion. Children love to twirl, spinning round and round until that sweet-sick feeling overtakes them and they collapse on the floor as the world keeps on going in circles around them. It is not surprising that *pirouettes* hold a special place in the vocabulary of a dancer; it is close to miraculous to see a dancer revolving around five or six times, or even ten times in the case of male dancers. Dancers' technical ability is often judged by the quality of their *pirouettes*.

Pirouettes, like the technique itself, have evolved through years of being practiced. Before dancing *sur les pointes* became part of the technique, turns were performed in a variety of positions with the working leg either extended, bent, or held in *cou-de-pied*. The preparation included a wind-up action rather like a skater's spin, as there was no necessity to perform a *relevé*. Like a skater, the head was held in one position in many of these *pirouettes*. Some teachers still favor the old way in *pirouettes* in *arabesque*, which lends a beautiful sense of serenity to that motion. The position of the supporting leg was a low quarter *pointe*, the heel just clearing the floor. This mode of execution was still being practiced by male dancers well into the fifties, thus allowing them to perform up to seventeen *pirouettes*.

As the technique evolved, demanding higher extensions, so too the performance of *pirouettes* also changed to include higher positions of the legs, such as high *retiré*. The height of the working leg as well as the position on *pointe* for the female dancer and a high half *pointe* for the male necessitated a different approach to the preparation. Additionally, the whipping action of the head—spotting—became an integral part of the turn.

Although the principles that apply to the execution of jumps also largely control the execution of *pirouettes*, two important features, balance and circular force, make it necessary to discuss *pirouettes* as a separate subject.

First the similarities. The actions leading to the *relevé* and spin as well as landing are the same as the actions required in a jump. There is a gathering of forces during the preparation, a pushing-off action preceding the *relevé*, a stretching of the limbs with the *relevé*, and a balanced landing. The arms provide some force and act as stabilizers. The spin, as in *tours en l'air*, is on the axis, the body perfectly aligned on all planes. If the *pirouette* is to finish on two feet, the heels are lowered to the floor at the same time, thus following the same rules as jumps in our first category. It is obvious that the application of weight transference is a major consideration in the execution of *pirouettes*.

Nevertheless, the action of spinning instead of jumping provides a very different kind of experience, relying heavily on the dancer's innate sense of balance.

To create a secure sense of balance, one must maintain a firm and steady contact with the floor. Thus the energy through the supporting leg is directed down into the floor, providing a firm support for the configuration of the body. Additionally, a "turning force" or torque is exerted against the floor to produce the spinning action. Dr. Kenneth Laws has analyzed in detail the action of spinning in his excellent book, *The Physics of Dance*. Drawing upon some of his findings, we examine the technical aspects of turns in classical ballet.

Theoretically, *pirouettes* can be executed in any position as long as they conform to the aesthetics of classical dance and the basic principles are honored. These principles are

1. When a *pirouette* is taken from both feet, equal pressure is needed from each foot to produce the necessary torque.

2. When the preparation is in fourth position, the center of gravity is placed over the leg which will become the supporting leg in the turn.

3. When a *pirouette* ends on both feet (either fifth or fourth position), the working foot closes in front for a *pirouette en dedans* and in the back for a *pirouette en dehors*. There are exceptions to this third principle. In a series of *pirouettes en dehors* to the same side, each spin closing in fifth before the next

one occurs, the working leg closes in front until the very last *pirouette*, which closes in the back. Additionally, choreographers are free to choose where the working leg will close, therefore the above is an academic rule which takes into consideration the direction of the spin and the most secure manner of concluding it.

4. The force arm is the one closest to the direction of the spin, (right arm for turns to the right, left arm for turns to the left), both arms need to assume their position as soon as the take-off has occurred.

5. The working leg must assume its position immediately after take-off.

6. The head stays behind as the turn begins and whips around in order to anticipate the progress of the body, arriving at the front before the body has concluded its revolution. The eyes focus on a spot and return to the same spot after the whipping action—spotting.

With these principles in mind, we will discuss some of the different types of *pirouettes* of the classical vocabulary.

Pirouettes en Dehors

The sequence of actions for *pirouettes* from fifth position is applicable, with modifications, to all *pirouettes*. If performed to the right, an *en dehors pirouette* will proceed as follows: *Demi-plié* as preparation, weight is equal on both feet. To the right, the right foot is in front, right arm in first position, left arm in second (fourth *devant*). The front arm begins the action on "and," opening toward the side but not as far as a true second position; simultaneously, both feet push off, the supporting leg (left) rises onto half or full *pointe* in a *relevé*, the working leg (right) goes immediately to a *retiré* position, the right arm returns to first and the left arm joins it. The head turns toward the front (stays behind) then whips to arrive, facing front before the body has completed the revolution. If the *pirouette* is to finish on both feet, at the completion of the turn, the right leg slips behind the left, finishing either in fifth or fourth position in the back. The arms open outward to a designated pose, usually the *offrande* position.

If the *pirouette* is taken from a fourth position, more weight is placed on the supporting (front) leg, although some pressure must be exerted by the back leg to create torque. However, the center of gravity is firmly placed over the front leg, pelvis, and shoulders aligned along that line. The back leg is straight except in *pirouettes* from fourth position which are executed with a partner; in this case the fourth is smaller and both knees are bent. The width of the fourth position is exactly the length of one's leg when extended in a *pointe tendue derrière;* lowering the heel to the floor gives the exact distance for maximum balance and efficiency for the push-off. At the completion of the turn the working leg slips back to finish either in fifth or fourth position.

The academically correct and most efficient manner of completing the turn is to close in the back. This method is founded upon physical principles. The working foot is placed where it will most efficiently break the impetus of the spin; therefore, the leg moves in the direction of the spin, acting as a brake when it makes contact with the floor.

The instant between the initial push-off, which is also the moment when torque is created, and the beginning of the spin is referred to by Dr. Laws as the moment of inertia. It is also the moment when balance is established. The importance of establishing balance at that moment grows in significance in proportion to the distance of the working leg from the central axis. In other words, simple *pirouettes* in a *retiré* position are easier to control than *grandes pirouettes* because of the closer configuration of the body mass to the center of gravity. During the spin, gravity exerts a backward force on the body. By placing the body mass in front of the line of gravity during the preparation and maintaining it forward during the spin, it is possible to counteract that force. Furthermore, the turning force, or torque, can also pull the body backward unless that force is directed toward the axis. Both the torque and the action of the arms can have the effect of pulling the body away from the line of gravity (even before the action of the spin exerts its backward pull). Therefore, establishing and maintaining balance (body mass forward of the line of gravity) is an essential component of turns. It must be pointed out that placing the body mass forward does not include leaning forward. Rather, it is an internal positioning while the body remains perfectly vertical. This positioning requires the dancer to press the body forward by uplifting the torso—the feeling is similar to standing in front of a wall and pressing up against it; the wall prevents the body from leaning forward even though all the forces of the body are directed that way. If an uncorrect positioning during the preparation is not detected, it can be deduced from the manner of finishing the turn—the dancer will, in all probability, drop the supporting heel to the floor prematurely, signifying that the weight was carried too far back.

The action from the arms also helps to maximize the torque generated by the feet. The front arm opening toward second capitalizes on the torque and helps propel the torso into the spin. Then the outward force of the arm is redirected toward the center of the body; the dancer feels it most directly as a force applied to the shoulder. The arm in second position does not produce force but acts to maintain balance; therefore, in simple *pirouettes* it is quickly brought to first position to join the force arm which returns to first after the initial opening to second. After that initial thrust the arms act as stabilizers and at the conclusion of the spin open outward to help break the impetus. Too much force from the arms can have the effect of throwing the dancer off the line of gravity, as noted above, but as long as the energy flow is redirected into the body, the force from the arms is a useful and necessary addition to the turning force generated by the feet.

The dynamics of *pirouettes* can be likened to the motion of a revolving door. The central pole of the door is contained within a rigid structure (the door). Pressure is applied in the direction of the motion at the farthest lateral point from the axis; this pressure starts the doors moving with optimal ease and efficiency. This physical fact explains why it is easier to start a *pirouette* from a fourth position than from a fifth; from a fourth position, the platform for balance is wider, allowing for more security during the preparation thus allowing the body to maximize the torque created by the feet. If the revolving door was made of soft rubber instead of steel and glass, pressure on it would make it buckle and sag. Similarly, a dancer assumes a "held" position. A distinction must be made between "held" and "rigid." A held position allows for subtle adjustments to occur even during the spin, while a rigid body cannot respond to changes or maintain balance. The dancer's axis is the central pole around which the rest of the structure revolves. The pelvis and torso act as a unit, fixed in their alignment just as the doors are fixed to the central pole. This placement provides a foil for the arms and the torque; the dancer creates a surface against which force can be applied.

It must be pointed out that male dancers need not spring up on *demi-pointe* as female dancers do onto full *pointe*. However, the downward pressure into the floor is the same whether one rises to *demi-* or full *pointe*, especially since a high *demi-pointe* position is favored today.

Pirouettes en Dedans

There are two types of *pirouettes en dedans:* one is called *fouetté en dedans* because the working leg opens to the side in a whipping action before it assumes the *retiré* position; the other one is without the *"fouetté."* Both can be taken from either fifth or fourth position with the working leg in the back. The preparation in fourth requires a greater width between the two legs than for *pirouettes en dehors*—approximately another half-foot. Nevertheless, the weight of the body is still placed squarely over the supporting front leg. This *pirouette* ends with the working leg in front either in fifth or in fourth position, or in poses in front like *attitude devant.* However, finishing in front is an academic rule, and just as *pirouettes en dehors* can end in a variety of poses, so can *pirouettes en dedans.*

The most common manner of executing *fouettés en dedans* from a fourth position (to the right) is: The right leg is in front in a *demi-plié,* the back leg extended with heel on the floor. The right arm is in front, the left in second (fourth *devant*). The left leg and the right arm open simultaneously to second position while the supporting leg is still in *demi-plié.* This is the moment of inertia preceding the spin. Then the working foot comes to a *retiré* position in front of the supporting knee and both arms rise directly to fifth as a *relevé* is executed on the supporting leg.

From fifth position, the working leg is in the back and opens sharply to second before coming to a *retiré* position. The supporting leg holds a *demi-plié* as the other leg opens to the side. For both turns the arms may be held in first or in fifth position during the spin. The most common finish to these turns is with the arms opening to second or to the *offrande* position. The *fouettés en dedans* can be likened to the fourth category of jumps, those that go from one foot to two. The turning force is generated, however, by both feet, since the working foot exerts pressure on the floor before opening to the side.

The series of actions described for *fouetté en dedans* is similar to the actions for *pirouettes en dedans* with the omission of the *fouetté.* In this case the working foot comes directly to a *retiré* in front of the supporting leg after the initial push-off. The arms generally are held in first position during the turn, although they can be raised to fifth. Most often the landing is into fifth position, working foot in front, although again the turn may end in a fourth position. This *pirouette,* like the *fouetté,* can start either in fifth or in fourth position.

Grandes Pirouettes

Grandes pirouettes follow the same principles as the two types of *pirouettes* described above except that usually the ending is on one leg with the other leg maintaining its original position. Additionally, the preparation in fourth is wider than the one for *fouettes en dedans*. The positioning for the preparation must place the body as close as possible to the position (angle of the leg *en l'air*) that will be assumed during the turn so that the least amount of displacement is experienced between the moment of take-off and the spin. By placing the legs in a wide fourth position, the center of gravity above the supporting leg, one is anticipating the height of the leg *en l'air* by the distance between the two legs in the preparation.

It is of the utmost importance that the position *en l'air* be assumed immediately; as soon as the push-off occurs, the working leg rises to whatever position the turn requires. Too often the dancer will perform a wind-up action, engaging in the spin before the working leg has reached its optimum height. This wind-up action jeopardizes the balance necessary for the *pirouette* and forces the dancer to make weight adjustments while in the spin. Dr. Laws (*Physics of Dance*, p. 55) observes, "When the leg is fully extended horizontally, it represents a large contribution to the total moment of inertia of the body, which makes the angular velocity (rate of turn) small for the magnitude of angular momentum that resulted from the initial torque." One adjustment that occurs among inexperienced dancers is an oscillation of the *arabesque* leg. This drooping Dr. Laws analyzes, and concludes, "When the leg drops, its mass is not so far from the axis of rotation, so the moment of inertia is decreased." This analysis provides a clear insight into the forces that a dancer must overcome in order to execute a clean *pirouette* in *arabesque*, and applies to all *grandes pirouettes*. Lifting the working leg directly into the position and maintaining the configuration during the turns is one way of solving this problem.

Pirouettes en Arabesque

In an *arabesque*, the weight of the leg is counterbalanced by the angled-forward body and even the arm. The tension established between the two extremities also serves to fully engage the torso. This tension between the two extremities is not a new experience; performing an *arabesque* correctly includes reliance on that tension as an integral part of the movement. We must add that the tension does not involve straightening the elbows; they remain soft in order to maintain the correct alignment. Additionally, the front arm remains firmly placed in front of the body. Not only does this positioning fulfill the aesthetic requirements of the pose, it also provides, by the squareness of the shoulders, the surface against which the dancer will apply force. Remember the frame of the rotating door.

The pressure of the feet into the floor, which generates part of the force for the turn, is twofold. On the one hand it is circular and on the other, it is a vertical thrust in order to raise the leg directly to the height required. The dancer experiences the *arabesque* position before the spin takes over and, through the experience, gains control. The front arm opens directly to the *allongé* position; the other arm assumes its position slightly behind the shoulder. During the spin, the position is maintained; the squareness of the shoulders, the position of the arms, and the leg in *arabesque* are all firmly fixed.

In the classical repertoire, *arabesque* turns are often performed in a series with a *plié* between each revolution. The *plié* serves two equally important functions. It helps the dancer regain balance and provides additional impetus, but only if the configuration of the body remains placed. The force from the *plié-relevé* is directed into the shoulder; if the shoulder is allowed to slip out of alignment then the force dissipates. The stability of the position of the body is, of course, a necessity in any type of *pirouette*, even those that do not involve a sequence punctuated by *relevés*.

Pirouettes en Attitude*

A *pirouette en attitude* is easier to perform than in *arabesque* because the configuration of the limbs is closer to the central axis. Nevertheless, the previous observation about assuming the required position immediately after push-off still applies. The action of the arms, however, is different for each type of *pirouette:*

1. For *pirouettes en dehors* taken from a fourth position *croisée*, arms in fourth *devant*: As the push-off occurs, the front arm

*The original *attitude* was inspired by a statue of Mercury by Giovanni da Bologna; the working leg in that pose is raised to the back. Thus, it is only necessary to qualify the pose when it is performed to the front—*attitude devant*. The term *attitude derrière* is superfluous.

rises immediately to fifth. Although the arm does not open to second, its function is the same as when it does—force is directed into the shoulder to add to the torque generated by the feet.

2. For *pirouettes en dedans* again from a fourth position preparation, arms in fourth *devant*: As the push-off occurs, the front arm opens to second and the other rises directly to fifth.

It is very important for the second arm to move directly overhead so as not to distract the balance nor exert a slowing down drag on the impetus that has been created. This action can be likened to rowing; the rower utilizes both oars equally to keep a straight course but if one oar should be kept simply in the water, the drag from it will affect the course of the boat. Similarly, the arm rising to fifth must do so with optimum speed and directness lest it distract from the momentum and balance.

Pirouettes à la Seconde

These *pirouettes* may be taken from either a second or a fourth position. In *en dehors* the arms are most commonly held in second during the turn; from a fourth position *devant* the front arm opens to second while the other arm remains in second; the working leg rises to 90 degrees immediately after the push-off. If the arms are required to be in fifth during the turn, the action of the front arm is the same as for *pirouette en attitude en dehors*—the arm rises directly to fifth, both arms reaching fifth position at the same time.

In *pirouettes à la seconde en dedans* the front arm opens to the side, then both arms rise to fifth. This *pirouette* is generally executed with arms in fifth. As in all previously described *pirouettes*, the working leg is raised immediately after push-off, but it is especially important in this case to maintain the turn-out of the working leg. Since the body is turning away from the working leg, the action of the working foot against the floor is inward. It is too easy to lose the placement of the foot and hence the whole leg at the moment of the push-off.

Grandes Pirouettes Sautillées

These *pirouettes* are executed with small hops in *demi-plié*, either in *arabesque* or in second position. In either case, the integrity of the position must be maintained throughout. In other words, the arms and working leg remain firmly placed and the torso fully engaged. The rapid heel lifts are the main feature of this *pirouette* with the ball of the foot maintaining contact with the floor. Since an enormous amount of force is generated by the continual spinning action, finishing the spin is a difficult task. Most often these turns are completed with a *pirouette* in *retiré*. The critical moment for maintaining control is at the instant when the working leg is brought in to the *retiré* position. However, there is technical help to break the force and redirect it closer to the center. Just before that action, the *demi-plié* is deepened, accented, with the body facing squarely front, then the leg is brought to *retiré* as the supporting leg rises to *demi-pointe* and the arms come to first position.

The *sautillés* are often coupled with *relevés* (described earlier in conjunction with *pirouettes* in *arabesque*). For example, eight counts of *sautillés* are followed by four turns with a *relevé* between each revolution. In this case it is important to perform the *demi-plié* linking each turn with the body squarely facing front.

Fouettés

There are two types of *fouettés en tournant*. The first was probably the original *fouetté* performed by Italian ballerinas at the end of the nineteenth century. This *fouetté* is executed by opening the working leg into second position before springing up again into the next spin as the working leg bends into *retiré*. The second type includes a *développé devant* followed by a whipping motion to the side before the *retiré* position is resumed.

The first type of *fouetté* is performed as follows: After the initial *pirouette en dehors* that starts the sequence, the working leg opens to second position at an angle slightly higher than 45 degrees, the arms open to second and the supporting leg comes down into a *demi-plié*. Then the dancer springs up again onto *pointe;* simultaneously the working leg returns to *retiré* and the arms return to first position as another revolution is executed. These *fouettés* are very rapid since it takes a relatively short time to open the working leg into second.

The second type of *fouetté*, more familiar to today's dancers, includes a *développé devant* and a *rond de jambe* to second between each revolution. As in the previous *fouetté*, the sequence begins with a *pirouette en dehors;* after the initial three-quarter turn (or one-and-three-quarter if a double turn is executed), the working leg opens to *devant* before the body reaches front. At that moment the arm closest to the side of the rotational direction is in first; the other arm opens to second. As the working leg travels to second, the front arm also opens to second; the supporting leg is in *demi-plié*. The supporting leg springs into *relevé* as the working leg is brought to *retiré* and both arms return to first position. After the rotation is completed and the body is almost facing front again, the same series of actions is performed. The head, of course, is spotting, and by that action also helps maintain balance. This *fouetté* is generally executed at 90 degrees.

The torque for both types of *fouettés* comes from the supporting leg. The circular force generated by the foot is aided by the action of the arms acting on the body and the whipping action of the working leg. For the whipping action to be effective, it is essential that the working thigh remain turned out and the lower leg must not go beyond second position in a kind of scooping action which destroys the alignment of the thigh. Again we need to remember the revolving door; when the thigh loses its turn-out, it also ceases to be part of the structure to which force can be applied in order to effect the spin.

In his analyses of the second type of *fouetté*, Dr. Laws remarks: "It is interesting that this stationary phase of the total movement takes about half the total time for a complete cycle of the motion, while the rotation takes place in the remaining half." The stationary phase is the moment when the dancer can regain balance, correct alignment, and create more torque with a steady push into the floor through the *demi-plié*.

As for so many of the classical movements, timing is of the essence. Even a slight break or hesitation may throw the dancer off center. With a large motion like the *fouetté*, timing acquires enormous importance. It is necessary both to not sit too long in the *demi-plié* nor to anticipate the *relevé*; both actions negatively affect the force needed to effect the next rotation. The *demi-plié* is relatively short during the going down phase and strong and sharp in the pushing-up action; the *relevé* is timed so that by the end of the rise the lower leg has reached the *retiré* position.

Another *fouetté* worth mentioning is the *en dedans* one. This version only opens to the side like the first type of *fouetté* and is usually performed in a sequence of *en dehors, en dedans, en dehors,* etc. The sequence begins with *fouetté en dehors* (second type). The working foot touches the back, then the front of the supporting knee during the rotation. It is then brought down in front of the supporting leg (*coupé*) in *demi-plié;* the other leg opens to the side and comes to *retiré,* touches the front, then back of the supporting knee before executing the *coupé dessous*. The original working leg then opens front and with the *rond de jambe*, executes the next *fouetté*. The *rond de jambe* is necessary since a lot of the impetus is lost in the execution of the *fouetté en dedans* and needs to be recouped with the *fouetté en dehors*. The exchange from one foot to the other must be as close to center as possible; the foot is brought down with the *coupé* motion to replace the foot on the floor under the body so that no extra shifting is necessary beyond the slight adjustment from one foot to the other.

A fascinating experiment in determining how much force is needed to turn and what role each part of the body plays is to perform *fouettés* without using the arms, keeping them akimbo or on the hips. Students will find that after the initial *pirouette* preparation, when the arms do indeed help create a good deal of the impetus, very little help from the arms is required. The force comes primarily from the torque of the feet acting on the shoulder (closest to the direction of the spin), and the action of the working leg. The arms are definitely stabilizers in this case and help preserve balance just as the head does with its rapid spotting motion.

The concepts of turning are generally introduced to students with *chaînés*. Executed in a first or small second position on *demi-pointe*, hands held on the hips and later in first position, the body performs half a turn with each change of weight from one foot to the other. The action of the head is emphasized as a prerequisite for spinning. Later, when the young student has acquired more control, *piqués en dedans* are introduced. Begin with a preparation in *pointe tendue devant*. The arms are in fourth position *devant* (front arm is the same as the front leg); the back leg pushes off, then assumes a *retiré derrière* position as the weight is transferred to the front leg on *demi-pointe* and the turn occurs. As the dancer steps up onto the front leg, the body turns a quarter turn and the front arm opens toward second; then both arms come to first position for the duration of the spin. After the body has performed three-quarters of a turn, the working leg is brought down (*coupé dessous*) to a *demi-plié*, the other leg extends to a 45 degree *en l'air* position *devant*, the arms are in fourth position and the next turn is executed. It must be noted that at the moment of the *piqué*, when the dancer steps up into the *retiré* position, the body is facing the line of direction. The *piqué* is executed frontally, and not sideways, a common mistake. The spotting is directed to the corner if the movement is performed on a diagonal or to wherever the line of travel is.

Although it is important that the student has gained enough control to maintain a position on *demi-pointe* before *pirouettes en dehors* are introduced, *chaînés* and *piqués* serve to habituate the student to the concept of spinning and establish the coordination between body and head that is essential to all turns.

We have examined the most common types of *pirouettes*, by no means exhausting all the possibilities or usages. However, the principles governing the execution of these *pirouettes* applies to all spins. To perform *pirouettes* takes good alignment, a strong *relevé*, coordination between arms, head and body, a clean spotting action of the head, and clear intent.

Pirouettes cannot be approached tentatively, yet the force generated by the arms and the torque of the feet must be used wisely lest it throw the dancer off balance. When all the parts act in harmony and coordination with each other, turning becomes a joy for performer and spectator alike.

Chapter 11

Pointe Work

Pointe work has had a checkered and at times an infamous history. Conceived as a means of emphasizing the ethereality of the female dancer, dancing on *pointe* soon degenerated into stunt dancing, culminating during the present century in tap dancing on toe and some of the precision antics of Rockette-style dancing. Nevertheless, *pointes*, when used in their romantic concept, place the dancer into the fantasy world so often portrayed in dance scenarios and add the flavor of otherworldliness to an already intricate technique.

The rise onto the toes did not occur until late in the eighteenth century. Most sources point to Charles Didelot (1767–1836) as the initiator of this innovation. In his historic ballet *Metamorphose*, produced at Lyons in 1794, the dancers made use of sophisticated flying machinery much in vogue at that time; it enabled them to stand on their toes fleetingly, before being whisked upward. This ballet was revived in 1796 at London's Drury Lane Theatre, being permanently christened *Zephyr et Flore* (or *Flore et Zephire*). He again mounted the ballet in St. Petersburg early in the nineteenth century.

Those who are variously credited with being the first to dance on *pointes* include Genevieve Gosselin (1791–1818), who stuffed her shoes to protect her toes; Fanny Bias (1789–1825), about whom Thomas Moore wrote, "she only *par complaisance* touches the floor"; Amelia Brugnoli, the 1820s *première danseuse* at Naples' San Carlo Theatre, who is reputed to have stood on her toes a full minute; Avdotia Istomina (1799–1848), who was admired for her interpretation of 'Flore' and who inspired Pushkin's verses: "With one foot resting on its tip,/Slow circling around its fellow swings"—ominously descriptive of *fouetté sur*

131

les pointes. But it was the delicate use of the *pointe* by Marie Taglioni (1804–1884) which opened for interpretation the half-world of nymphs and spirits.

In the relatively short time between the first use of *pointes* without machinery at the beginning of the nineteenth century and the great neo-classical ballets of Petipa (1818–1910) and Ivanov (1834–1901), the shoe had hardened and the technical intricacies had multiplied. By the late nineteenth century, *pointe* work had become not so much a pause in space as a series of intricate steps performed entirely on the toes. This mode is exemplified by the fairy variations in the prologue of the *Sleeping Beauty*, choreographed by Petipa in 1890. Although these variations are jewels of characterization, the corruption of the concept lies just below the surface. From the hops, walks, and runs on *pointe* in these dances to what we know as tap dancing on toe is not an illogical evolution.

While Taglioni, wearing the soft slippers of her day, had to darn the tips of her shoes to harden them, less than a century later Anna Pavlova (1881–1931) had to soften the blocks of her shoes in an attempt to recapture the quality of otherworldliness characterizing the use of the *pointe* shoe by Taglioni. Pavlova presented the dancer again as an elusive creature, able to transcend the laws governing mere mortals.

Classical ballet lends itself to the exploitation of the art through the more spectacular aspects of the technique. Ballet audiences have come to expect physical prowess from the performers, be it a series of high vaulting jumps from the *premier danseur* or thirty-two *fouettés* from the ballerina. Dancers indulge themselves and their audience by specializing in one form or another of technical skill. As a student in the fifties, I witnessed performances where the ballerina, having attained balance in *arabesque* or *attitude* on *pointe*, held the pause for as long as she could while the conductor repeated the same musical phrase over and over again.

This tendency to play on the physical aspect of dance, sometimes in violation of aesthetic synthesis, is not new to our age. Jean-Georges Noverre (1727–1810) waged a lifelong battle against the idea that dance was mere *divertissement*. Michel Fokine (1880–1942), among his many ideas and innovations, deplored the practice of applauding a singular piece of dance virtuosity in the middle of a ballet, an act often intruding on the artistic whole. His search for truth in motion and integrity of the art has given us many fine ballets which, instead of glorifying the physical prowess of man, pay tribute to the sensitivity of the spirit. Isadora Duncan (1878–1927) railed against classic technique, calling it unnatural and distorting. Martha Graham (1894–1991), while rejecting the classic form, created a technique no less arduous and precise; but, unlike some of her classical counterparts, she never lost sight of the central motivation for motion or action. This insight makes her a much truer follower of Fokine's philosophy than many classical choreographers.

Fortunately for the art, ballet history can boast of many choreographers who, following Fokine's example, have used the *pointe* selectively as an integral part of the character being depicted. Roland Petit in his ballet *Le Jeune Homme et la Mort* (Paris, 25 June 1946) choreographed a long sequence of *bourrées sur les pointes* for the girl when she returns as death to lead the young man over the rooftops. The stiffness of the motion emphasizes the coldness of the character and her remoteness from all living things. *Idylle* (Paris, 2 January 1954), a ballet by George Skibine, tells of the antics of a white mare and a black stallion. The equine quality comes beautifully alive in the high kicks and strutting *pointe* work with which Skibine chose to portray the movements of the mare. Leonid Massine has also used *pointes* judiciously. In *La Boutique Fantastique* (London, 5 June 1919), the parents and children who come to purchase dolls wear character shoes, much like street shoes, while the dolls are on *pointe*, indicating subtly the fantasy aspect of these characters.

Although *pointe* work is now an integral part of the classic technique, the choreographic use of the *pointe* is of course left entirely to the discretion of the choreographer; he is at liberty to use them in any ballet of any period. Thus, preparing girls for proficiency on the toes today must include a familiarity with the various modes of execution from the Romantic, through the neoclassic, into our own age, when modern contractions performed on toe are not uncommon.

The modern *pointe* shoe has a very hard block, squared off at the tip. The block extends over the phalanges and a third of the way up the foot, giving the necessary support to the knuckles and toes and guaranteeing a long, unbroken line to the foot. The shoe comes in varying degrees of hardness, of width to suit the breadth of the foot, and of vamp length to enclose and mold the top of the foot. The shoe has three soles: one outside, usually made of thin leather; one inside, made either of cardboard or leather; and one between these two, a thick leather tongue extending from the middle of the heel to just under the ball of the foot and shaped rather like a flattened spoon. This in-between sole is the vital core of the shoe. It must be supple but not brittle, must bend with resilience, and must answer exactly to the arching of the foot.

Dancing on toe may be more accurately described as dancing on the metatarsal arch. The construction of the *pointe* shoe protects the toes and forces them to stretch out, not under. The weight of the body is supported by the intrinsic muscles of the foot and the longitudinal arches, but it rests on the metatarsals. The toes must not buckle under, but rather extend to form a gentle curve. The block of the slipper to some extent prevents this buckling under, as does the thick inner sole of the shoe. When that sole loses its resilience, the shoe is broken and can no longer support the foot. It is preferable for the neophyte to select a shoe with a high vamp (three or four inches) in order to insure the correct use of the instep as well as to minimize the stress on the joints of the toes.

The ideal dancer's foot is rather stubby, with all the toes almost the same length. This structure provides a broad base for equilibrium. Yet as long as the big toe is not inordinately longer the dancer should not have any major problems. Far more important are the degree of arching that the foot can achieve and the strength of the many muscles that support the arching. A child with a great deal of mobility in the ankle will have to be careful neither to roll inward toward the big toe nor to roll outward toward the little toe. Rolling toward the little toe (supination) will produce a sickled foot and a weakened ankle. Rolling toward the big toe (pronation) may lead to an enlargement of the plantar metatarsophalangeal, the ignominious bunion, and an undeveloped longitudinal arch. A child with little mobility in the foot and ankle will have to work hard to develop a good line by stretching the ligamentous connections, while taking care that the foot does not pronate.

Correct position of the foot will cause the muscles leading to the little toe to be shortened and the ones leading to the big toe to lengthen. The ability to work with the foot in such a position is a prerequisite to *pointe* work. But before considering the muscular requirements for *pointe* work, the readiness of the bones to accept all that weight should be discussed.

Bones have varying rates of ossification. Epiphyses are layers of cartilage whose presence in the bone indicates that it has not completed its growth. As growth ceases the cartilage gradually becomes ossified; when closure is completed no more growth can occur. Some epiphyses do not completely ossify until the twentieth or even the twenty-fifth year. The bones that concern us here are in the lower extremities and bear the burden of supporting the body's weight. The femoral head, the lower end of the tibia, as well as the numerous bones of the foot, normally begin the process of ossification in the fourteenth year. This process is not completed until the twenty-first year (a little earlier in females).

From these figures, we can deduce that putting girls on their toes is a fairly hazardous undertaking unless the musculature has been developed enough to protect the integrity and alignment of the joints all the way down the leg. We should remember that the force of gravity always acts in a vertical direction. If the body is aligned from head to foot, the dancer will experience the force in one vertical plane. But if the body is misaligned, gravity will pull on it in several different planes, and various extraneous muscular contractions will be necessary to maintain balance. Thus it is that malformation and permanent damage can result if a child is put on *pointe* too early or with insufficient preparation.

It takes approximately four years to develop the proper musculature to rise on the toes. If a child begins dancing at age eight, she will be ready to don *pointe* shoes around her eleventh or twelfth year. Even if the child starts dancing earlier (which is not a good idea), she should not begin *pointe* work much before that time if damage to her skeletal structure and internal organs is to be avoided. We only have to think of the old Chinese custom of binding the foot, which stopped its natural growth, to realize how malleable and vulnerable a young body is and how carefully it must therefore be nurtured in its growth and development.

From the earliest years of training, the foot must remain aligned to the ankle. In *relevé* or slow rises onto *demi-pointe*, the weight is placed more toward the inside of the ball of the foot (big and second toes) to avoid that sickling which occurs frequently when the outside of the foot stretches more than the inside. When slow rises have been mastered, the child is ready to *relevé* with a little hop or spring, which duplicates the action necessary for the rise to full *pointe*. Slow rises should not, however, be discontinued; a slow rise develops strength and control and should remain a part of training.*

By the time a student starts *pointe* work, she has mastered many of the exercises at the *barre* in two versions: on a flat foot and on *demi-pointe*. The exercises which lend themselves to both versions include *battement fondu*, *frappé*, *ronds de jambe en l'air*, *développé*, *petit battement*, and some *grand battement*. The stance on a true *demi-pointe* is

---

*One of the most strengthening exercises for both ankle and phalanges is found in the striking-out action of *battement frappé*. The ball of the foot grazes the floor before toes and ankle are fully extended.

very close to the one required for full *pointe* insofar as the weight distribution and muscular involvement are concerned. On *demi-pointe* the platform (the ball of the foot) is wider and provides a steadier base for equilibrium. But if the child is well placed in all respects, then the rise onto *pointe* is only an additional skill to be practiced and mastered without undue stress or damage to the joints.

The very first exercises on *pointe* are done facing the *barre*, using both hands for support. To begin, all movements should be on two feet: *relevé* in first and second position, *sous-sus* in fifth position, *échappé* into second, *glissade* and *assemblé sur les pointes*. When these steps can be executed with straight knees, a well-placed pelvis, and no strain in the shoulders, *bourrée* can be introduced, followed by *jeté*, *relevé* on one foot, and *pas de bourrée piqué*. When the child holds her back well, has no wobble in the ankle, and has mastered the slight spring necessary before the rise onto toe, she can use one hand on the *barre* instead of two. *Échappé* into fourth position, *sissonne en croix*, *piqué* and *relevé* into a *retiré* position as well as *arabesque* and *attitude* should be done before simple movements are attempted in the center without the support of the *barre*.

Once in the center, all steps learned at the *barre* should be practiced. In time, *retiré passé*, all the varieties of *pas de bourrée*, *soutenu en tournant*, and *temps liés sur les pointes* can be added to the vocabulary. When *retiré passé* can be executed correctly, *pirouettes en dehors* and *en dedans* can be introduced. Preparation for *pirouettes* on *pointe* is the same as for *pirouettes* on *demi-pointe* and begins with a *relevé* from fifth or fourth position into a *retiré*. The exercise is taken first in quarter turns, then half turns, and finally full turns. From one *pirouette* to two is an easy transition if the student is well placed, and it requires very little additional force. A child who is afraid of turning must have her attention drawn away from the idea of the spin, and instead be told, for example, to put her energy into the *relevé*, or into spotting, or into keeping her working foot pointed. Any diversion will do as long as it distracts her from the spin itself, which can then proceed without the hindrance of unnecessary tension.

The feet and legs are strengthened by repeated *relevés*, on two feet and on one. The number of *relevés* on one foot must increase only very gradually, as a tired muscle will not be able to support the alignment of the structure and real injury may result. Ten minutes of *pointe* work at the end of class is sufficient for first-year students. The time may be increased gradually as the vocabulary grows so that by age fifteen a whole class can be done entirely on *pointe*.

Some exercises besides the classic ones are useful for strengthening a particularly weak ankle or bringing back mobility after an injury. Flexing and stretching the foot at the ankle, being careful to emphasize the stretch of the inside top of the foot leading to the big toe, is both gentle and effective. Making circular motions with the foot, while the leg is kept still, is a sure way to increase mobility. The toes also can be exercised in isolation, by flexing and extending them at the knuckles, which brings into play both the plantar and dorsal muscles of the foot as well as some muscles of the calf. All those exercises that consist of isolated movement in the lower leg can be done sitting on the floor with legs outstretched. Another extremely effective exercise should be performed standing with the weight on both feet: making sure that the metatarsals bear equal weight throughout the exercise and that neither pronation nor supination occurs, the plantar muscles of the longitudinal arch are contracted and released. This exercise strengthens the keystone area of the foot which bears the weight of the body both on flat foot and on *pointe*. A strong longitudinal arch prevents too much stress in the metatarsals and phalanges of the toes.

All exercises at the *barre* prepare in some way for the eventual execution of particular movements on the toes. The principles governing the execution of all classic movements apply to *pointe* work as well. *Pointe* work is an evolution of the classic technique, however, and is in no way a technique in its own right. A well-placed dancer, whose musculature is ready to deal with the various problems presented by steps done on toe, will be able to solve the difficulties involved by following the same logical process used in understanding an unfamiliar step. How is the weight distributed? Where are the areas of stress? How strong is the attack at the beginning of the movement? How do variations in timing affect the execution of the step? Although the teacher will answer these questions, when first introducing *pointe* work, by demonstrating the movement and by giving corrections, advanced students can improve their execution by periodically reapplying the basic precepts of classic dance as they relate to their technical proficiency.

Little girls are usually eager to start dancing on their toes, but responsible teachers will restrain their impatience, knowing that irreparable harm can be wrought if the bones and muscles are not ready to accept the burden. The harm is not limited to feet and ankles alone; the femoral head in the acetabulum can also be injured, although the damage may not be immediately apparent. Those children who attend ballet classes once or twice a week for fun should never be put on *pointe* at all. If they should, at age thirteen or fourteen, suddenly discover a strong urge to become serious dancers, it is not too late to start *pointe* work, provided that the basic training has been sound and that the back, legs, and feet are properly developed.

Chapter 12

Style

*One goes out onstage with a well-prepared technique, a knowl-
edge of how to present that technique in its most refined form.
But beyond that, what counts is the ability to be free on the stage,
to* dance. *When I prepare a role, I naturally learn the steps
first; however, I try to find the appropriate style from the
beginning, and then rehearse the steps in it. As a young dancer
I had a quite developed, secure technique, but my sense of style
was often appalling. I now know that style is what gives blood
and color to the bones of the piece, the technique. It is of
the utmost importance to work very hard to make technique
and style one.*

Mikhail Baryshnikov
Baryshnikov at Work

In a broad sense, style is the sum total of individual
choices. The ways in which a person walks, talks, and dresses are
aspects of his whole being, and each is conditioned by such factors as
cultural milieu, peer pressure, and the expectations of superior or model
figures. Initially style is shaped by an unconscious process, both in the
individual and in the arts, which at least on one level reflects the age. In
dance, style is directly influenced by the traditions that have shaped the
art, by the cultural milieu where it flourished, by the authorities
expounding the technique at the time, and by the physical make-up of
the interpreter.

When we examine classical ballet style, we are forced by
traditionally accepted standards to see in a particular way. Well-
established ideas of form govern the execution of this art. Thus it may be

said that all expressions of a classical dancer are channeled through a censor's vision which makes them conform to the standards of classicism. Thus too, because classical style subordinates individual choices, historical reasons must be sought to explain them.*

Even as we can trace the basic steps of the classic technique to the court dances of the sixteenth century, so can we recognize in our own perception of the beautiful some standards of that age. In the writings from that period, there are clear, although infrequent, injunctions related to the deportment of the performers. Moral and social virtues governed the style of the dance and were even reflected in the carriage of the dancers. The man was proud, chivalrous; he sought glory for himself as much as for king and country; his movements were resolute, masterful, noble, and elegantly dignified. The woman was modest, gracious, and charming; her movements were soft, compliant, full of gentle grace. In *Orchesography* (1588), one of the first books to deal with the technical execution of court dances, Arbeau writes in great detail upon the intricacies of the footwork and the musical phrasing, with interjected references to the countenance that dancers should exhibit:

> A cavalier may dance the pavane wearing his cloak and sword, and others, such as you, dressed in your long gowns, walking with decorum and measured gravity. And the damsels with demure mien, their eyes lowered save to cast an occasional glance of virginal modesty at the onlookers.

Drawing extensively from Arbeau's work, Dolmetsch, in her *Dances . . . 1450 to 1600*, writes thus about the arm movement:

> Should he dance without a hat, he can make moderate gestures, drawing the hand inward and upward for the first and second beats, and lowering it outward in a graceful curve for the third and fourth beats.

This pre-classic description would only arouse our historical interest if we did not recognize in this simple gesture the foundation of today's *port de bras*. Elsewhere in his book, Arbeau indicates that the arm movements blended elegantly with the footwork, that the gestures were rounded and sober, that arms were held slightly away from the body with motion mostly confined to the lower arm, below the elbow. Most

---

*A comprehensive historical survey is beyond the scope of this work. We have limited ourselves to some major events or personalities that have shaped the development of the classical style as we know it today.

steps were performed *terre à terre,* drawing attention to the floor patterns; a lilting use of the flat foot, *demi-pointe,* and bending of the knees gave grace and continuity to the movements.

The early ballets relied heavily on the court dance vocabulary. Whether we call them mummings, masquerades, or *ballets comiques,* they consisted of interludes or *entrées* linked, often by declamations in verse, around a unifying theme such as the myths of antiquity. Geometric designs and *tableaux vivants,* together with singing, dancing, and music, culminated in impressive spectacles designed to glorify allegorically a king, foreign dignitary, or other personage being honored.

It was not until the reign of Louis XIV that what we may properly call ballet moved from the private court into the public theatre. Even then it retained its elegance of style and theme and was still largely inspired by Greek and Roman myths. In 1661 Louis XIV established the Academie Royale de Danse, which opened the door to the vocational and professional dancer. To this event we owe the great technical advances in dance and its eventual emergence as a distinct theatre art. Yet the courtly connection was not severed. Rather, the court dances took on the ordered aspects of planned choreography.

In *La Contredanse* Guilcher speaks of dances performed at court in the seventeenth century:

> It is governed by an intelligent order which hardly accommodates liberty and spontaneity. Between the step and the pattern a harmonious balance has been established which compliments one through the other. Everything is subject to a conscious control; everything is conceived for visual appreciation and subordinate to an exigency of style.

In this passage Guilcher could as easily be describing the many choreographed entertainments that Jean Baptiste Lully (1632–1687), composer to the king, had created in collaboration with Bensarade (1612–1691) and Beauchamp (1636–1705). The mythic-epic style continued to be in vogue in France through the first part of the eighteenth century, as evidenced by the compositions of Jean-Philippe Rameau (1683–1764). As was customary, dance usually played only a small part in the total spectacle.

By mid-century individual adaptations of the traditional ballet attire allowed the body freedom to perform ever more complex steps. Marie Camargo (1710–1770) shortened her dress and scandalously revealed her calves; she also adopted a heelless shoe to perform the *entrechat quatre,* an innovation she is credited with originating. Her rival, Marie Sallé (1707–1756), was the first to dispense with the cumbersome paniers and the confining bodice. These changes permitted more freedom and greater expressiveness in the upper body.

In 1760 Jean-Georges Noverre (1727–1810) published *Lettres sur la Danse,* advocating the principles of *ballet d'action,* mimed-drama or story ballet unaided by poetry or song. At this point dance alone carried the dramatic message. Noverre had to resort to lengthy program notes in order to explain the plot of his historical ballets, and he devised mimed sequences which replaced the spoken word of earlier productions. While Noverre denounced the subordinate role dance played in most spectacles, Auguste Vestris (1760–1842) forged ahead with technical improvements. Two concurrent schools of thought emerged: mimed dramas, still relying heavily on the *divertissement* or danced interludes which Noverre favored; and the pure display of technique with little concern for the story line which Vestris practiced.

At the end of the century the French Revolution transformed the mores and standards of society and could not but have had an influence on dance as well. Following the trends of fashion in dress styles, costumes became filmier, lighter; men partnered women on stage; and, of more consequence, the audience was no longer limited to aristocrats, so ballet began to have a wider popular appeal.

Out of the ferment of the eighteenth century a new style appeared. Charles-Louis Didelot (1767–1837) combined and refined the philosophies of Noverre and Vestris into the Romantic style: mimed dance, danced mime. A simpler story line almost dispensed with program notes; now dance alone could carry the plot; emotions and moods could be transmitted by the steps themselves; acting became an integral part of dance. The courtly structure of the technique was retained, while the boundaries of expression and technical execution were enlarged. Ballet found inspiration in less exalted subjects. Gods from Olympus made way for shepherds, fairies, peasants, and sylphs who brought a simpler gesture to the technique. Marie Taglioni (1804–1884) personified the period, sometimes referred to as the golden age of ballet. Her purity of line and ethereal quality introduced poetry of motion into a dance that was concerned to a great extent with technical displays of skill.

During the nineteenth century the artistic capital of the dance world gradually shifted to Russia. When Didelot arrived in St. Petersburg in 1801, he reorganized the teaching at the Imperial Ballet School. He laid the foundations for the distinctively Russian style, and he was followed by Danish, Italian, and French masters. Foremost among them were Christian Johansson (1817–1903), Marius Petipa (1818–1910), and Enrico Cecchetti (1850–1928). It is remarkable that despite the rapid evolution of dance technique during the eighteenth and nineteenth centuries, classic dance retained much of its original courtly character. This continuity can be explained in part by the neo-classical revival initiated by Marius Petipa, who dominated the artistic and technical development of dance in Russia for fifty years. The classical repertoire of today still consists largely of his overwhelming contribution.*

Petipa made use of many aspects of dance from preceding ages. His prince and princess characters displayed the noble qualities of the gentlemen and ladies of the court. But they were enriched by the Romantic qualities of forlorn longing in the male and of demureness, playfulness, and innocence in the female, not to mention the otherworldliness of the sylph-derived characters. The calm, unchallenged superiority of the male was matched and balanced by the girlish yet commanding charm of the female.

These aspects of classical characterization are magnificently exemplified in Petipa's *Sleeping Beauty*. In the Rose Adagio of the first act the young princess is wooed with dignified grace by four suitors. There is a hint of simplicity in the demeanor of this princess, a manner surely borrowed from her peasant cousin. Toward her suitors she is gracious without familiarity, a woman who will not be compelled to make a choice. Toward her father, the king, she is girlishly obedient while begging not to be forced into a choice. In the dream scene of act two she becomes an ethereal vision, the remote wili or teasing nymph. In the third act Grand Pas de Deux she is totally royal, serene, and fulfilled, dancing with her prince to the delight of the entourage.

The dignified posturing, much admired in the time of Louis XIV and imitated by Petipa, can still be seen in the head and arm carriage of today's dancers. The most basic pose of a classic dancer must be imbued with an aristocratic understatement. The uplift of the torso elongates the waistline, preserving the illusion of artificial stays and bones; the deliberate rounding off of all movements of the upper body enhances the calm, effortless quality that forms the base for all other characterizations. Each neophyte tests herself, however unconsciously, against these qualities. Although most contemporary ballets require

*Classical in the purest sense of the word, although the full range of a classical repertoire includes the Romantic ballets of Dauberval, Perrot, Saint-Léon, and those twentieth-century ballets which utilize the technique.

neither the spontaneous simplicity of the peasant character nor the commanding nobility of the princely one, they often utilize the gestures of either or both.

The manner of the court of Louis XIV is hardly comparable to our current mores, yet three centuries later, classic dance, using those manners, still speaks intimately to a wide and disparate range of people. If any cultures now share in the traditions of seventeenth-century Europe, they certainly do not do so to the exclusion of their own enduring and evolving traditions. Yet there is a universality in the language of dance that hardly needs verification. It is a transcendent matter which age cannot wither nor custom stale. Doubtless the expression of man's timeless striving to explore the fantastic or imaginative side of his nature and to communicate his dreams in the joys of untrammeled motion is to some extent inherent in the classic technique.

In the eighteenth century Noverre had cried out for reform. At the beginning of the twentieth, Michel Fokine (1889–1942), a product of the Russian school, was able to put his innovative ideas to the test in the company formed by Serge Diaghilev (1872–1929). Fokine, as chief choreographer in the early years of the Ballets Russes de Diaghilev, formulated basic artistic principles which have guided and influenced nearly all subsequent choreographers. Today no theme seems unsuitable for dance so long as the integrity of the subject matter, the time, and the character of the music are observed. In today's plotless ballets we have extracted the character from the gesture. While leaving the rationale behind, we have still kept the pose.

Because Fokine opened the doors to a new, broader perception of beauty in movement and Isadora Duncan awakened others from preconceived forms and ideas, contemporary choreographers have a wide choice in the application of the technique. They may present, as John Cranko did in *Lady and the Fool* (1954), a Romantic theme with the undeniable charm of a Romantic treatment; or they may explore the darker side of human nature, as found in Ibsenesque dramas such as Antony Tudor favors. They may resort to comedy or even to simple poetic renditions of a single thought. Or, like Sir Frederick Ashton in *Symphonic Variations* (1946), they may apply the classic style in all its purity; in this ballet the movements and patterns are so closely related to the music that one watches the musical phrase and listens to the dance.

Classic style, in our day, does not doom either choreographer or dancer to one particular theme or characterization; it is rather the starting point for a great many movement expressions. It is the language that formulates a statement. The statement may take many forms from the mundane to the transcendent, from the concrete to the abstract, without veering from the classical syntax of gesture. The structure of the language determines the form of the statement. Thus the gesture of the classic dancer, steeped from the earliest years in the thought process of classicism, cannot but be dependent on the technical aspect of that discipline. Style inheres in the movement, and the movement is governed by tradition.

There are of course numberless individual differences and personal idiosyncrasies among choreographers, even between companies, but to contrast the merits of choreographic genre or even to compare the styles of ballet companies or the qualities of individual dancers would lead us away from our central concern. Our purpose is to examine the universality of the classic style, not to delve into the particulars which distinguish usage and interpretation.

Although the ultimate manifestation of the classic style is the performance, it is in the classroom—within the boundaries of the technique and before the incorporation of creative interpretation—that style is inculcated. The old masters left us a rich legacy not only in the exercises that condition the body for the arduous poses which the art demands, but also in the terminology of the technique which clearly points to particular interpretations of almost all the classic steps. These terms are not abstract ideas to be debated; they are concrete signposts which any child can understand. Coupled with some knowledge of our heritage of courtly carriage and dignified bearing, these principles constitute the foundation of the classic style. Pure, correct, unmannered execution of the steps leads to this specific style.

The rigors of classic training impose qualities of simplicity, fluidity, and economy of gesture on all motion. Training so shapes dancers that even in their unmonitored motions, such as walking or standing, their manner becomes somewhat altered and standardized. Even the physiognomy of dancers is usually different from that of other performers, as if the discipline had whittled away any excess flesh to reveal the essence of their beings. It could be said that a classical dancer does not choose a style, but rather that a style is imposed on the dancer's mind and body and that it rules every motion.

Our forefathers came early to the conclusion that the leg's range and beauty of movement are greatly increased by an outward rotation. They perceived that motion is aesthetically more pleasing when executed in this fashion than when the legs are parallel. They explored the expressiveness of hands and feet and the range of the body's mobility, linking the poses and moves to the emotions they endeavored to convey. Thus there slowly emerged a complex technique which developed in specific ways the range of movement available to the human structure.

Steps and movements were gradually discovered to convey meaning; then exercises were invented to aid the body with the execution of these moves. Fitting style—the socially and/or artistically accepted way to comport oneself—dominated the choice and tone of these moves. The dancer of today has a rich heritage: a technical vocabulary to be mastered and a style that distinguishes classical ballet from other dance forms. *But because that style no longer reflects familiar social values, it too must be learned.*

The dancer will learn, in the course of training, not only where to put her feet, but how the arms and head complement each motion. She will understand, for example, that a focus over the front shoulder allows her to maintain a visual-emotional dialogue with the audience. She will rely on the placement of the upper body (uplift of the torso and relative roundness of the arms) to define her statement and place it in the context of classic form. These considerations are the mechanics of style and are inseparable from the mechanics of technique.

The goal of every student of ballet is to come as close as possible to the ideal classic form. To this end there must be complete concentration during class just as much as during performance, for it is in class where we nurture and refine our style. This concentration flows in two directions: An inward flow allows the dancer to internalize the corrections of the teacher and to experience every movement, and an outward flow enables her to be aware of space and to direct her motion therein. Good style is the result of a *heightened awareness of the connotation of one's every mood and action,* however minute they may be. When dancing on stage, the dancer projects her energy outward in order to allow the audience to share in the experience of the dance. (This too can and should be simulated even in class.)

Fernau Hall speaks explicitly of this matter in his *Olga Preobrazhenskaya:*

> There is something that needs stressing at the present time, when there is a strong tendency to treat dance training as a set of mechanical exercises that, if done correctly in the right order, produce the proper result after a few years. In fact they tend to produce dancers who are little more than robots, not interpretative artists—as they must be if they are to make their proper impact on the stage, as soloists or as corps de ballet dancers. It is a great mistake to think that technique is something that is taught in class quite separately from feeling or

artistry; the dancer must learn how to feel each movement, how to be an artist, from the very beginning of training. By the time he or she enters a company, it is much too late to learn that dancing is an art. This was exactly the attitude of Preo herself, who may have gotten it directly from Cecchetti. Elvira Roné has quoted Cecchetti as saying, "That which one has not done in the ballet school will never be picked up there—on the stage. . . . The foundation must be laid during the period in the ballet school."

Theatrical dance is not an inward experience to be hoarded and hidden, but rather a sharing and a giving one. Even as a small child is taught how to share with his playmates and curb his instinctual selfishness, so too must a dancer learn this principle. The ability to share the emotional content of a movement is as integral a part of execution as technique. Unfortunately this aspect of the technique can often be overlooked. Repeating the same basic movements every day, as dancers do, quickly forms habits. Familiarity sometimes breeds indifference and blunts the edges of perception. Deviations from the ideal, which are the result of individual physical or perceptual traits, are allowed to creep in. The execution becomes at best expressionless, at worst unnecessarily flowery and mannered.

It is easy to confuse style with mannerisms, yet nothing could be more destructive of true style than irrelevant idiosyncrasies. Mannerisms are usually an outgrowth of some kind of personal compulsion or compensation, sometimes acquired during training and often used as a masking device for deficient technical ability. If mannerisms go unchecked, real problems in execution may be hidden, and progress, both technical and artistic, may be inhibited. It can be likened to splashing on cologne to hide the fact that one has not bathed—the scent cannot altogether or for long disguise the odor of dirt and sweat.

Most often, style-related mannerisms take the form of unnecessary hand and wrist movements which distort the simplicity of the classic line while adding nothing positive to the feeling of the movement. A flopping wrist is a sign of bad style as surely as a sloppy fifth position is a sign of inadequate or careless technique. Viewed in this context, style is as much a habit-forming discipline as is the strictly technical acquisition of skills. If the habits acquired in the classroom conform to the principles of good posture, to the directness of the classic statement, and to the simplicity of the basic gesture, then the technique and style of the performer become a malleable, coherent vehicle for expression. If, on the other hand, arbitrary divergences are allowed to creep in, then the clarity of the statement becomes obscured. The edges of execution are blurred until it is no longer possible for the performer, so enveloped in habits, to recognize the meaning and import of any given motion.

The acquisition of a technique and a style is motivated by one single need: to become a proficient interpreter. Technique is the tool. Style is the qualifying factor, revealing not only the influences that have shaped the performer but also the individual's psyche, which interprets the information from the start. There is a certain latitude possible in the classic technique that allows divergences in interpretation; but only those artists who have acquired a complete familiarity with the language can take liberties with the syntax. These divergences are a choreographer's prerogative, but they do not belong in the classroom during the formative years of the student. During those years, style is defined by the purity of line and the harmonious coordination between gesture and step.

Dance is a total discipline. The art, and thus its style too, encompasses the physical, the emotional, and the intellectual aspects of a person. This idea is well condensed in Buffon's famous definition, *"Le style est l'homme même"*—style is the man himself. Even as style can be conveyed by the physical gesture and, as such, is as much a part of training as learning the steps, it is also a frame of mind. It is a quietness of the soul which allows the dance to flow through and take possession of the performer and the spectator alike.

Chapter 13

Classical and Modern Dance

Dance began in worship, ritual, and magic.* Man spoke to his gods in gesture and created visionary states through motion. He delved into his soul to find his hopes, fears, and aspirations. These feelings inspired his dances. The tradition of a two-way dialogue—one directed inward, the other outward—is as old as dance itself. Although some religions and some primitive peoples have retained dance as part of their ritual, most dance has gradually lost its heavenly connection.

In the western world dance has assumed an increasingly secular character, and at least since the Renaissance it has been recognized as a distinct art form whose predominant role is to entertain. Instead of speaking to his god, man now addresses his fellow man. Regrettably, a great deal of the old personal introspection seems to have been lost. This change of focus has been accompanied by the formation and subsequent growth of a complex technique. Only those dancers who can transcend their technical achievements, however, can fully experience their art inwardly and fully communicate that experience outwardly.

---

*The classic statements on this theme are Curt Sachs, *World History of Dance*, and Franziska Boas, *The Function of Dance in Human Society*. Although the claim for religious ritual is a pervasive one, the story of dance origins is shrouded in prehistory and cannot be documented with certainty. The best recent scholarly study of the oldest of the arts is Anya Peterson Royce, *The Anthropology of Dance*; on the present discussion, see her concluding chapter and her superb bibliography.

Although there are many forms of dance, for several centuries the prime theatrical dance form in Europe was the balletic. In recent times, however, a major schism has occurred. Some dancers felt that the content and form of classical dance could neither adequately express the concerns of the age, nor fully explore the possibilities in artistic movement. Isadora Duncan rejected the balletic form and resumed a divine dialogue on her own terms. Unfortunately, she did not formulate a technique that would enable lesser mortals to follow her lead. That task was taken up in various places, but the most enduring exponents of modern dance were in Germany and America. Chief among the moderns were Mary Wigman (1886–1973), her colleague Hanya Holm (1898–), and Kurt Jooss (1901–1979) in Germany; and in America Ruth St. Denis (1880–1968) and Ted Shawn (1891–1972) and their students, Martha Graham (1894–1991) and Doris Humphrey (1895–1958), and others such as José Limón (1908–1972) and Charles Weidman (1901–1975). These vanguard artists not only choreographed extensively but also created a distinctive new vocabulary of motion.

At first glance the principles governing modern dance may seem to be totally opposed to those governing ballet. Whereas the classic dancer strives to deny the laws of gravity, the modern dancer uses gravity as an important component of movement. This difference in fact accounts for the chief qualities of mass and weight that distinguish the two techniques. The ideals of classical beauty, discussed in the previous chapter, preclude the use of certain positions in the composition of classical dances, whereas modern dance has no such traditional considerations limiting its gesture. Thus a full range of gesture is available to the modern dancer which concomitantly expresses a potentially larger and more specific range of ideas and feelings. Movement in modern dance is explored for its power to express. Emotional impulse is transformed into kinetic energy causing movement to develop organically. The energy radiates outward from one's center, be it a physical center of gravity or a conceptual center of motivation. Vocabulary is created to suit the thought. Still, as suitable expressive movements have been found, modern techniques have increasingly and inevitably become more formulated. Some modern systems are now grounded in a cycle of training as strict as the balletic one. In many instances this established vocabulary is used in choreographic works.

By contrast, in classical ballet the motivation for the movement is the step itself. The steps, linked into *enchaînements*, govern the use of space. Isolated *variations* are constructed from these *enchaînements;* they act as interludes in the tradition of the *Ballet de Cour* and show off the technical dexterity of the performers. In the story ballet, the plot provides a pretense for linking the variations into a unified spectacle. Thus classic dance today is in a situation similar to the one deplored by Noverre in the seventeenth century, and Fokine's complaint in the 1920s that the form dominated the content seems generally applicable five decades later.

There are many ballet choreographers who use the technique discreetly in all its wealth, but for many the selection of movement is purely arbitrary. Two opposite examples come to mind, the rechoreographing of two classics, Baryshnikov's *Nutcracker* and Balanchine's *Coppélia*. Baryshnikov loses sight neither of the story line (however feeble it might be) nor of the essential character of the players. He never succumbs to the lure of spectacular leaps or lifts if they do not suit the context or idea to be expressed. His version of the ballet is a coherent, sensitive whole, culminating in the final scene between the Prince and Clara which is a jewel of characterization. In the movements devised by Baryshnikov, Clara remains throughout the little girl dreaming a fabulous dream; she never steps outside her childlikeness; the choreography establishes the character and sustains it. The final scene is especially touching because of the delicacy with which Baryshnikov selected the lifts and steps to portray the characters within the situation.

In direct contrast, Balanchine in the last act of *Coppélia* (the first two acts were staged by Danilova) appears to disregard many of the usual connections between movement and meaning. For example, the variations performed by three female soloists, bearing the titles of Dawn, Prayer, and Spinner, seem in no way to reflect the spirit of the titles in the quality of their movements. Even if one does not expect the subject to be treated in the graphic manner of the Royal Ballet version, it is something of a jolt to see Dawn leaping hysterically around the stage, Prayer kicking her legs aggressively above her head, and Spinner effortlessly flitting about. But Balanchine groomed his public to accept inconsistencies as virtues. In a recent interview in *Ballet Review*, P. W. Manchester remembers Balanchine's *Cotillon*, which was choreographed in the early 1930s: "It was typically Balanchine in that there was an idea rather than a plot, and he didn't even develop the idea." Later, talking about *Concurrence*, dating from the same period, "A girl came on and sort of drifted around the stage, and she hadn't anything to do with the rest of it." From the tone of the interview, one does not sense a negative connotation in these observations.

Because Balanchine handled the movement characterization masterfully in so many of his works (*Apollo*, 1928; *The Four Tempera-*

ments, 1946), one presumes it is by conscious choice that he disregarded those more sobering aspects of the choreographic process. When a master takes liberties with the rules, we acclaim his daring and control; unfortunately it has led many imitators mistakenly to believe that by stringing together a few well-chosen *enchaînements*, intercepted by some spectacular lifts and leaps, they can create an artistically whole ballet.

This approach is in part the cause for the modern movement's rejection of many aspects of the classical technique and for the climate of mutual exclusion which has often prevailed. Yet, little by little, the barriers separating classicism from modernism are being removed. Increasing numbers of dancers are versed in both techniques, while many choreographers freely supplement the classic form with modern concepts. Because of this blending of the modern and classical idioms, it has become apparent that modern dance can make some valuable contributions to the training of classical dancers; the reverse has already been proved true. As this book has been concerned with the development of the classical dancer, our concluding observations are limited to the influence of modern dance on ballet.

Ballet is usually taught by rote. Students are asked only to reproduce the movement as accurately as possible; they are not encouraged to think. This emphasis often results in a loss of awareness of the process involved in the execution of any motion. If classroom exercises are performed mindlessly, the experience becomes routine, the movement loses its content, and only the shape remains. In this area ballet can especially benefit from the modern approach.

The modern concept of a *center* as a motivational hub for all action provides a *raison d'être* for movement that otherwise might seem to be arbitrary. Coordinating a movement only serves in part to create harmony between limbs and body. The other parts required to make an integrated gesture are intent, which is intellectual in origin, and feeling, which is the gut-response triggered by intent. These two components can be further qualified and thus more easily experienced. Intent determines the attack. It sets the level of energy at which the phrase is going to be performed. Feeling refines the raw energy and introduces a focus into the dynamics. Intent and feeling are unified into a single force which directs and colors the dynamics of movement. Movement approached in this manner cannot remain arbitrary, cannot be a collection of *pas* strung together by connecting steps. It becomes the logical expression of a thought, an idea in the broadest sense, encompassing intellectual as well as sensory motivation. Some classical dancers are familiar with the concept of a center, but most do not accord it as much importance as their modern counterparts do. In addition, there are several distinctly modern concepts which are worth investigating from the classical point of view.

Doris Humphrey developed the idea that dance takes place between a fall, when the body gives in to gravity, and a recovery, when it asserts its will against the gravitational force. José Limón added a new dynamism to the concept by substituting "rebound" for recovery. The classic dancer never gives in to gravity with the abandon displayed by modern dancers, yet the mechanics of weight transference, discussed earlier, are closely linked to the effect of gravity on motion. Although equilibrium is highly regarded in classic dance, it is nevertheless only a transition from one point of imbalance to another, not a static state to be sought for its own sake. The spectator may perceive the sustained balance as arrested motion, yet the subjective experience, in its full context, is a continuous one leading to renewed overt activity. Thus for classic dancers, as well as for moderns, dance takes place between these equilibrant states: the suspension or balance using gravity to support the action (recovery—rebound) and the passage through a reorganization of weight (fall) to make the next moment of suspension possible.

Martha Graham's credo of contraction and release as the motivation underlying motion is yet another useful concept, one which is fundamental to all movement. While Humphrey's emphasis relates the dancer to his space, Graham deals more with body attitudes. Her technique relies on a deep contraction to create a circularity in the body (rather like a tight coil) which gives force and direction to the release. Release is not a loss of tension but a diffusion of energy through the body and limbs outward, a feeling familiar to the classic dancer. Although the deep contraction has no counterpart in the classic technique, variations of it are experienced in many movements.

Any action is preceded by a gathering of forces, a drawing inward toward one's center, like a snake coiling before it strikes. Energy is concentrated and then released with a specific force and direction. The movement is anticipated intellectually but experienced only in the rhythmic moment of performance. Thus a contraction induces an awareness of the center which leads to an awareness of the process that shapes any action, an awareness arrived at prospectively rather than retrospectively.

Presumably owing in part to some need to justify their distinctness, the moderns have generally done more prospective intellectualizing about their art. More than the classicists, it seems to me, they have studied the process for itself. In contrast, the classical art, which evolved more slowly, has often learned its techniques *ex post facto* from innovations originated by pioneering performers rather than from thoughtful consideration of the process.

Most modern techniques stress sensory awareness. The pose is merely the final manifestation of the process or progression of a movement. The means are as important as the end. For example, the extension of one leg until the toes are fully pointed (*battement tendu* or the modern *brush*) can be a sensory, even a sensual, experience. The foot works against the resistance of the floor, drawing strength from the downward press preceding the heel's lift-off; the leg reaches out, bringing sensations to the back of the knee; the instep's gradual arching transmits the tension down to the toes. When the tautness has reached its climax, tension begins to ebb away and the foot returns gratefully to a closed position.

The simplest *port de bras* can also be experienced in this way: a slight uplift of the torso precedes the motion of reaching forward and opening to the side in an unbroken flow; the breath is drawn in as the arms travel from *bras bas* to first position; the arms proudly open to the side as the breath, which created a certain tension, is exhaled. The dancer has established a relationship between his physical boundaries and the space he occupies. A modern dancer would say that he has defined his space. Most classic movements, however, have no inherent emotional content. The dancer experiences them on his own terms. Yet the joy to be derived from any motion is an important element of that experience and is, in fact, a measure of the dancer's total commitment to the action.

Both classic and modern dancers face many of the same problems. For each, dance is a theatrical expression which has to conform to the limitations of stage space in its attempt to communicate. Each technique uses the human body as interpreter. Thus before vocabulary is considered we are confronted by the living instrument and the conditions that control its natural rhythm: the beat of the heart, the measured intake and exhalation of breath, the contraction and release of individual muscles. In another context, Tom Robbins related human action to life itself:

> Actions, like sounds, divide the flow of time into beats. The majority of our actions occur regularly, lack dynamism and are unaccentuated. But occasional actions . . . are accentuated due to their intensified stress. When an accentuated beat is struck in relation to one or more unaccentuated beats, there arises a rhythmic unit. Rhythm is everything pertaining to the duration of energy. The quality of a man's life

depends upon the rhythmic structure he is able to impose upon the input and output of energy.

Dance may be defined in these same terms—that is, as a unit of flowing action with a rhythmic structure controlling the quality and duration of energy input and output. Technique institutionalizes the rhythmic structure into a language. The language lives only as long as it communicates the dynamism it represents, adapting to and evolving with its attendant opportunities and needs.

As we witness the evolution of dance, we can see the growing influence of modern dance in many choreographic works in the repertory of leading classical companies. Likewise, we can detect the influence of classicism in many modern class structures through the development of a more varied technical vocabulary. Today many choreographers demand that the dancer be versed in both techniques. An understanding of both forms is important even for the dancer whose specialty lies in only one field.

Glossary

The following pages are intended as reference points and aids in visualizing particular movements. The stick figures move from left to right, simulating a dancer's own mirror image. The reader therefore needs to face the drawing and will in most cases use the right leg to execute the *pas*. When a small arrow is found at the tip of a limb, it indicates the line of movement of that limb; a long arrow below the figure represents a traveled step.

When a step begins in fifth position, the forward foot is indicated by being drawn a little below the back foot. When the position is fifth in the air, the forward foot is drawn a little longer than the other. The double lines for the body are used only when it seemed particularly important to indicate that the body is facing *croisé* or *effacé*, a curved line indicating the chest, a straight line being the back. The same system is used for the head, the curved line indicating the face and the straight line indicating the back of the head.

This glossary does not attempt to describe all the steps of the classic vocabulary, but illustrates only those that are discussed in the text. A more complete list, often with more detail, is to be found in Gail Grant's *Technical Manual and Dictionary of Classical Ballet*, a source which I have occasionally consulted but which on some terms should be used with discretion or in consultation with other interpretations.

Arabesque. A basic balletic pose, generally taken in profile. The working leg is extended straight behind, the supporting leg may be straight or on *demi-plié*. The hips and shoulders are square to each other and to the line of direction.

ouverte

1st   2nd   3rd

croisée

1st   2nd   3rd

(a) *Arabesque penchée:* Tilted *arabesque*. Like a seesaw on its fulcrum, the body tilts forward in relation to the height of the working leg. The back is strongly arched.

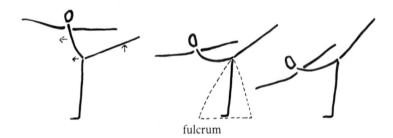

fulcrum

(b) *Pirouette en arabesque:* A turn in *arabesque* position. It can be done *en dehors* or *en dedans;* preparation for both versions is usually from the fourth position. Push-off is from both feet, arms and legs assuming the position for the turn immediately. This *pirouette* is the only one in the classic repertory that does not use the head to spot.

en dedans   *en dehors*

Assemblé. To assemble or place together. Fourth category jump. (See chapter 9.)
(a) From fifth position, the working leg slides out and is thrust to a 45 degree angle in the air; as the leg is extended, the supporting leg pushes off; the legs join before landing in fifth position. The movement can be done *devant* or *derrière;* when executed *à la seconde* it is taught both *dessus* and *dessous.*

dessus

and   one

(b) *Assemblé battu.* Beaten *assemblé.* From a thrust into second position, the legs beat in the air before the landing. *Dessus:* the working leg beats back and then front. *Dessous:* the working leg beats front and then back.
(c) *Assemblé sur les pointes. Assemblé* on *pointe.* Instead of springing up in the air, the dancer assembles the feet on *pointe* in fifth position.
(d) *Assemblé en tournant. Assemblé* with a turn. Usually preceded by a *pas de bourrée;* as the working leg is thrust into second position, the body

revolves in the air. This *assemblé* is generally done *dessus*, the body turning *en dedans*, and it is often beaten.

(e) *Assemblé volé*. Flying *assemblé*. Preceded by either a *glissade* or a *failli*, this *assemblé* travels in the air. It can be beaten: front, then back, then closing in front before the landing; this *assemblé* is called *entrechat cinq volé* by the French school.

Attitude. A pose inspired by the statue of Mercury by Giovanni da Bologna; its first use is credited to Carlo Blasis. The supporting leg is straight, the working leg is raised to a 90 degree angle, or higher, and bent; the foot and the knee remain aligned with each other on the same horizontal plane.

effacée or *ouverte*   *croisée*

(a) *Pirouette en attitude*. A turn in the *attitude* position. Preparation for the turn is usually in fourth position, either *croisé* or *effacé*. The push-off is from both feet, the working leg and arms assuming the position as the *rélevé* is executed. It can be done *en dehors* or *en dedans*.

en dedans   *en dehors*

Balancé. A rocking step resembling a waltz, consisting in three parts of alternation of balance. The first movement is a step down into *demi-plié* (on the right leg), the left leg is on the *cou-de-pied derrière*. The second movement is onto *demi-pointe* of the left leg, the right leg extended softly downward. The third movement is a step down to *demi-plié* on the right foot; the left foot is again on *cou-de-pied derrière*. The first step is traveled; the two others are *en place*. *Balancé* may be done in a series, alternating legs; it may travel *en avant*, *en arrière*, or *de côté*, or it may be executed *en tournant*.

and   one   two   three

Ballonné. Bounced, like a ball. Third category jump. Usually preceded by a *coupé*, the working leg extends in a battement to 45 or 90 degrees while the supporting leg pushes off. The working leg bends to the *cou-de-pied* as the landing occurs. It can be done *devant*, *derrière*, *dessus*, or *dessous*. It can also travel *en avant* or *en arrière*, in which case it is done in a series, the working leg repeatedly extending into *battement* accompanied by the spring of the supporting leg.

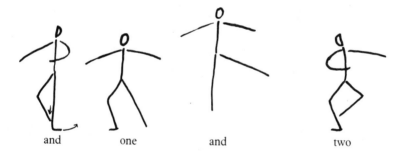

and   one   and   two

Ballotté. Tossed, like a boat on the waves. Third category jump. A jump from one foot to the other involving the upper body in a rocking motion forward and backward over the supporting leg.
(a) With straight legs (Russian). Preparation is a *dégagé derrière;* the dancer springs into the air, the back leg (left) joins the right leg. The right leg then opens to *effacé devant;* the body leans back as the landing occurs. The dancer immediately springs up again, the right leg joining

the left; the left leg extends to *effacé derrière* as the body leans forward
and the landing occurs.

and   one   and   two

(b) With a passage through *raccourci* (Italian). This *ballotté* begins with
the same preparation as the straight-legged one. However, this time as
the spring occurs, first the left leg then the right are drawn into a high
raccourci position; the right leg extends in a *développé devant*, the body
leaning back as the landing occurs. This is followed by the next spring,
the right leg then the left being drawn into the *raccourci* position. The left
leg now extends into *développé derrière*, the body leaning forward as the
landing occurs.

and   one   and
         devant

two   and   one
derrière   *devant*

Brisé. Broken, shattered. Fourth category jump. A low, traveled, and beaten *assemblé*. Throughout the execution of the step or steps, the body leans over the working leg. *En avant* (right foot back in fifth position): the right foot opens to a 45-degree angle in *écarté devant* direction; the left foot pushes off and beats back then front. *En arrière* (left foot front in fifth position): the left foot opens to an *écarté derrière* direction, the right foot pushes off and beats front then back. The traveling is in the direction of the opening leg, usually executed on a diagonal.

and   one
right leg beats front—then back

(a) *Brisé volé.* Flying *brisé*. Third category jump. In this movement the working leg describes a low (22 degrees) *rond de jambe* before the beating occurs; the initial supporting leg then becomes the working leg, executing in its turn the *rond de jambe*. The motion finishes on one leg, the working leg either on the *cou-de-pied* or straight *devant* then *derrière*.

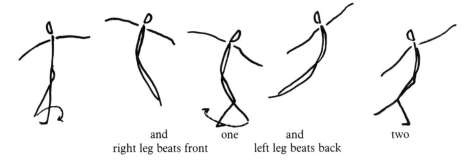

and   one   and   two
right leg beats front   left leg beats back

Cabriole. Caper, like a goat's jump. Third category jump. In this step the working leg opens straight out; the supporting leg pushes off and beats underneath the working leg, propelling it higher. The landing occurs on one leg. This jump can be quite small with the working leg opening to a 45 degree angle, or it can be executed with a high extension and a correspondingly high jump.

(a) *Cabriole ouverte.* The working leg remains extended up after the landing has occurred; the next jump has to be taken from the same supporting leg.

(b) *Cabriole fermée.* The working leg closes fifth after the landing has occurred. The next jump can be taken from both feet. *Cabriole* can be done in all positions and with a single or a double beat.

effacée devant fermée

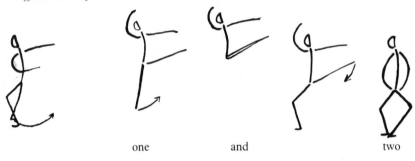

| one | and | two |

Chaîné. Linked like a chain. A series of turns with the feet in first position, weight shifted rapidly from one to the other with each half turn. The head spots over the front shoulder, looking in the direction of travel. It can be done in a diagonal or *en manège.*

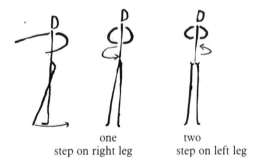

one
step on right leg

two
step on left leg

Changement de pied. Changing the feet. First category jump. A straight up and down jump, from fifth position to fifth position with a change of feet in air. *Changement* encompasses all the variations in height; it can be done with the tiniest of springs off the floor or as a high, suspended jump.

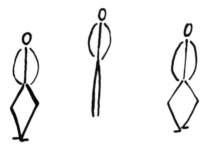

Chassé. Chasing one foot with the other. The right foot slides forward to a fourth position; then with a slight spring off the floor, the left foot draws up to it in the air, and the right foot opens to fourth as the land occurs. The movement is continuous. *Chassé* can be done in *croisé* or *effacé* traveling forward or backward; it can also be done from side to side.

en effacé

and   one

Coupé. To cut. A sharp preparatory step used as a link between steps like *jeté* and *assemblé* or before a *ballonné*. One foot is raised to the *cou-de-pied* and brought down sharply to replace the other foot. It can be done *dessus* or *dessous*.

and

Croisé. Crossed.

Demi. Half. As in *demi-plié*, or as in *demi-hauteur*, half height, generally referring to arms held below the second position.

Derrière. Behind.

Devant. In front.

Dessous. Under, closing a step in fifth behind.

Dessus. Over, closing a step in fifth in front.

Échappé. Escape, to break loose. First category jump. This movement has two distinct parts: (1) opening the legs outward from fifth position; (2) bringing them together again in fifth. Both feet open an equal distance from the line of gravity in the opening outward, either into second position or into fourth. Each part involves a jump.

à la seconde

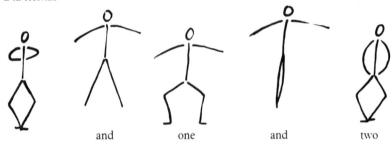

and   one   and   two

(a) *Échappé sauté.* From fifth position the dancer springs into the air, opening the legs into second or fourth position. He then jumps up again, bringing the legs together to finish in fifth position.
(b) *Échappé sur les pointes.* This *échappé* is done with a spring onto *pointe* in the open position, returning to fifth position in *demi-plié*.

Écarté. Spread wide.

Effacé. Erased, shaded.

Élancer. Darting. Qualifies an allegro *enchaînement*. Cecchetti's sixth basic movement in dancing.

en quatrième et à la seconde

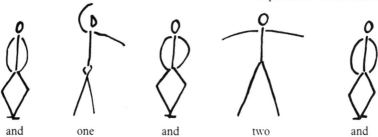

and	one	and	two	and

Emboîté. Fitting in. Third category jump. A light, springing step, from one foot to the other, the jump finishing with one foot on the *cou-de-pied*. Generally done in a series *en tournant*. With each spring, the dancer executes half a turn.

en tournant

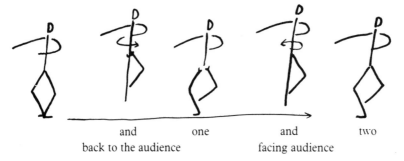

	and	one	and	two
	back to the audience		facing audience	

En arrière. Traveling backward.

En avant. Traveling forward.

En dedans. Inward. Can refer to a circular movement of the leg executed from back to front or to a *pirouette* done toward the supporting leg.

En dehors. Outward. Can refer to a circular movement of the leg executed from front to back or to a *pirouette* done away from the supporting leg.

En face. Facing the front (the mirror in the studio, the audience in the theatre).

En tournant. Turning.

Entrechat. Cross-caper. A straight up-and-down jump in which the dancer crosses the legs, each in front and then behind the other, the desired number of times. Each crossing counts as two movements. Even-numbered *entrechats* finish on both feet: *entrechat deux* or *royale* springs from both feet, beats front to finish in the back. *Entrechat quatre* beats back to finish in front. *Entrechat six* beats back then front to finish in the back. Odd-numbered *entrechats* finish on one foot, the other leg on the *cou-de-pied*, in front or behind: *entrechat trois* beats front, finishing on the *cou-de-pied* back; *entrechat cinq* beats front then back and finishes on the *cou-de-pied* front; *entrechat sept* beats back then front and finishes on the *cou-de-pied* back. All *entrechats* can be reversed, in which case the back leg is thought of as the working leg.

Étendre. To stretch. Cecchetti's second basic movement of dancing.

Failli. To fall short. Second category jump. A preparatory step providing attack to a variety of jumps and steps on *pointe (assemblé volé, fouetté)*. Begins in fifth position, right foot front. Push-off is from both feet. Legs are held close together until maximum height has been reached, the body turning slightly to effacé. At the height of the jump, the left leg opens to a low *arabesque effacé*. The landing is onto the right leg, the left sliding through first position to a large fourth *devant croisée*. The front leg is in *demi-plié*.

and   one   and

two

Fermé. Closed. Qualifies some jumps which usually finish in an open position, such as *jeté fermé*.

Fouetté. Whipping. A strong whipping movement of one leg accompanied by a half or full revolution of the body.

(a) *Grand fouetté sauté*. Third category jump. Preceded by a *failli*, the right leg extends in a *grand battement devant*. Pushing off the supporting leg, the dancer turns away from the working leg in the air and lands in first *arabesque*. This can also be done with a full or a half revolution in the air. Following the first *fouetté*, the dancer swings the working leg through first position to *grand battement devant* and executes a turn in the air *en dedans* while the whip is taking place. The landing is on the same leg.

(b) *Grand fouetté sur les pointes*. This movement is the same as *fouetté sauté* but with a spring onto the *pointe* instead of a jump.

sur les pointes or sauté

and   one   and   two

facing upstage

(c) *Fouetté rond de jambe en tournant*. A female dancer's showpiece. Usually executed as a series of turns on one leg, it consists of a whipping movement of one leg accompanied by a turn on *pointe*. The working leg goes from *devant* through the second position into a high *raccourci;* the supporting leg springs on *pointe* as the working leg passes through the second position. This *fouetté* may be done *en dehors* or *en dedans*.

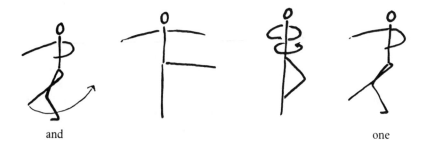

and   one

Gargouillade. Gurgling or rumbling. Third category jump. Usually preceded by a *coupé*, this step is similar to a *pas de chat*. It involves a *double rond de jambe en l'air en dehors* with the front leg followed immediately by a *double rond de jambe en l'air en dedans* with the back leg as the jump is in progress. The back leg ends in front, and thus the step can be repeated to the other side.

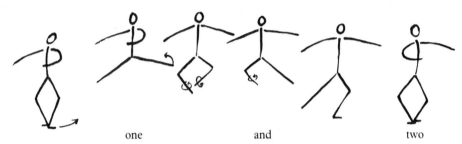

one   and   two

Glissade. Slide or glide. A linking or preparatory step. The working leg slides out to a *dégagé;* weight is transferred to it in order to allow the other leg to point and slide into fifth position. The quality of *glissade* is determined by the context of the *enchaînement:* slow and sustained in *adagio*, sharp and fast in *allegro*. It can be done with or without a change of feet and can travel *en avant, en arrière, or de côté.*

and   one

Glisser. To slide or glide. Cecchetti's fourth basic movement of dancing.

Jeté. Thrown movement. Third category jump.
(a) *Grand jeté en avant.* A high jump from one leg to the other usually preceded by a *pas couru* or a *glissade.* It begins with a *grand battement* to the front, pushes off the supporting leg, and lands on the front leg with the back leg in *arabesque.* It travels forward in the air.

(b) *Grand jeté en tournant*. *Grand jeté* in which the legs pass each other in the air while the body is revolving. Usually preceded by a *pas de bourrée couru*. The first leg does a *grand battement devant* (the dancer is facing upstage); the second leg kicks while the first leg is still in the air, the legs passing each other in the back as the body revolves to face front again. The landing is in *arabesque* on the first leg.

one   two   three   and

one
back to audience   two   three

(c) *Petit jeté.* Little *jeté.* This can be done with or without an extension to the side. Without the extension it is similar to *emboîté,* the working leg being lifted to calf height. *Petit jeté* can travel forward with the legs lifting in the back, or can travel backward with the legs lifting to the front. With an extension it is done *dessus* or *dessous.*

and   one   and

(d) *Jeté dessus.* *Jeté* over. From fifth position right foot back, the right foot slides out to the side to a 45 degree angle; the left foot pushes off and bends to finish on the *cou-de-pied derrière.* The landing is onto the right foot.

(e) *Jeté dessous.* *Jeté* under. This is the same movement as *jeté dessus* but this time the front foot opens, and the *jeté* finishes on the *cou-de-pied devant.*

Ouvert. Open.

Pas de basque. A step derived from the national dances of the Basques. Taking three distinct counts, it can be done *en avant* or *en arrière.*

(a) *En avant.* From fifth position right foot front, *demi-rond de jambe par terre* from front to side with the right foot; the weight is on the left leg, which is in *demi-plié.* Transfer the weight onto *demi-plié* on the right leg, while the left leg extends to *pointe tendue* and, passing through first position, steps forward into fourth position. The weight is transferred to the left leg as the right leg is extended to *pointe tendue derrière.*

en avant

one   two   three

(b) *En arrière*. The same movement is executed as for *avant*, but the back leg extends to *pointe tendue* followed by a *demi-rond de jambe par terre en dedans;* the other leg passing through first position steps back into fourth, the front leg extending to *pointe tendue devant*. It can also be done with a spring *(sauté)*.

and   one   two

Pas de bourrée. A step originating in country dances. This movement involves three steps and can travel in any direction. There are many types of *bourrée*. Following are the most common.

(a) *Pas de bourrée devant:* From fifth position right foot front. The right leg opens to second position just off the floor; left leg is in *demi-plié*. Right leg returns to fifth position front, both feet on *demi-pointe*. Left leg steps out to second position. Right leg closes in front fifth position. (Close front, step side, close front.)

(b) *Pas de bourrée derrière:* Close back, step side, close back.

(c) *Pas de bourrée dessus:* Close front, step side, close back.

(d) *Pas de bourrée dessous:* Close back, step side, close front.

dessous

and   one   two   three

(e) *Pas de bourrée couru: Bourrée* running. This can be described as a balletic run in three counts usually preceding a high jump. It can also be performed on *pointe* in fifth position traveling forward, backward, or sideways. It may also be done with feet in parallel position traveling forward or backward.

Pas de chat. Cat's jump. Third category jump. Fifth position, right foot back. The right foot lifts to a high *retiré* as the left bends to push off. After the push-off it bends to a high *retiré*. The legs pass each other in the air as the left leg travels up to *retiré* and the right travels down. Landing is on the right leg with the left foot closing in front a moment after the landing.

and   →   one

Pas de cheval. Horse's step. Third category jump. It has the light, nervous quality of a thoroughbred horse pawing the ground. It begins with the right foot pointed *devant*, the leg slightly bent at the knee. With a *petit développé*, the right foot scratches the floor while a little spring is executed on the left leg. The motion can be repeated continuously, or stepping onto the right leg, executed with the left. It travels forward with each spring. It may also be done on *pointe*, the body leaning slightly forward over the legs.

hop-step   hop-step

Pas de ciseaux. Scissors step. Third category jump. A high jump where both legs kick straight in front one after the other and pass each other in the air, the second leg brushing through first position into *arabesque*. It is usually preceded by a *pas de bourrée couru*.

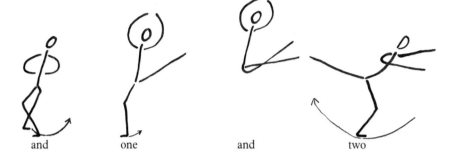

and one and two

Pas de papillon. Butterfly step. Third category jump. Preceded by a *tombé* into a wide fourth position, weight on the front leg; one leg then the other kicks back, passing each other in the air, the second leg sliding to the wide fourth position. The arms undulate from side to side like butterfly wings while the body curves back with each successive jump.

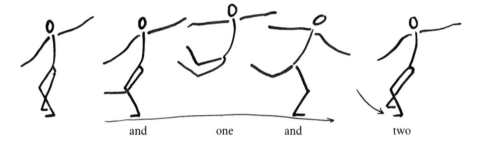

and one and two

Piqué. To prick with the toes as with a needle. A sharp motion onto a full or *demi-pointe* of one leg, the other leg raised to any given position. (a) *Tours piqués.* The sharp motion onto *pointe* is accompanied by a turn, the working leg is in a *retiré* position. It can be done *en diagonale* or *en manège.* A *coupé* is used between turns.

en dedans

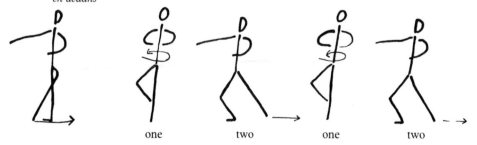

one two one two

en dehors

and   one   and

Placement. To be placed. A well-placed body is one that is correctly aligned, without useless tension, to allow free motion. Standing in first position, the feet should be placed firmly on the floor, the weight of the body falling evenly over the longitudinal arches, toes flat, heels on the floor, weight equal on big toe, little toe, heel. Legs straight, calf and thigh muscles taut but not grabbing, allowing the outward rotation to occur in the hip socket. Hips square and even; buttocks held but *not* tucked under. The spine is lengthened, ribs allowed to hang on the spine in their natural curve, not pulled upward. Shoulders free of tension but held back, balanced over the hips; chest open. Neck and head aligned with the spine. Head erect. There should be a general lengthening feeling, pushing down through the legs and up from the waist.

Pirouette. Whirl or spin. A controlled spin on one leg, the other raised in a variety of positions. *Pirouettes* usually begin with a push-off from both feet, the supporting leg rising to a full or a *demi-pointe* while the working leg assumes the desired position, in *retiré, arabesque, attitude, seconde,* and so on. The turn may finish on both feet or in any position on one leg. The head stays behind and then whips around ahead of the body—spotting— at each revolution. The turn is either *en dehors* (outward) away from the supporting leg or *en dedans* (inward) toward the supporting leg.

en dehors

and   one   two

en dedans

and   one   two

à la seconde

en dedans   *en dehors*

Plier. To bend. Cecchetti's first basic movement of dancing.

Posér. To place down. A soft stepping onto one leg, as in *posé en arabesque*.

Relevé. A rise. A strong rise or spring up onto half or full *pointe*. It may be done on both feet or on one in a variety of positions.

one   two   one   two   one   two

Relever. To raise. Cecchetti's third basic movement of dancing.

Renversé. Turned upside down. Preceded by a *tombé* into a deep fourth position in *croisé* and a *coupé* with the back leg; the front leg describes a *grand rond de jambe en dehors*, finishing in *attitude* or in *arabesque croisée*. The body leans forward over the supporting leg, the back strongly arched; this movement is accompanied by a *relevé* on the supporting leg and ends with a *pas de bourrée en tournant*. For *renversé en* *dedans,* the action is quite different. From a high *développé* in second position, the working leg is brought sharply into a high *retiré,* the body leaning sideways over the working leg while the supporting leg is in *demi-plié;* this movement is accompanied by a swivel toward the supporting leg and finishes in a high *développé* in second position on half or full *pointe,* the body leaning away from the working leg.

en dehors

en dedans

Retiré. To take away or withdraw. One leg lifts to the height of the knee of the supporting leg, which remains straight.

Retiré sauté passé. Withdrawn jump passing from front to back or vice versa. First category jump. The push-off is from both feet; the working leg comes up to the knee, passes it, and the landing occurs on both feet. This can also be done with a *relevé* onto half or full *pointe.*

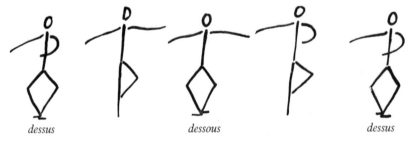

dessus   *dessous*   *dessus*

Saut de basque. Basque jump. Third category jump. Preceded by a *chassé*, a *pas de bourrée couru*, or a *glissade*, this jump involves a turn in the air. A *grand battement devant* is executed at the moment of push-off, the supporting leg coming in to a *retiré* position for the revolution in the air; the landing occurs on the leg which did the *grand battement*, the other leg remaining in *retiré*. This step is often done in a series on a diagonal.

en tournant

and   one

Sauter. To jump. Cecchetti's fifth basic movement of dancing.

Sissonne. Named for the creator of this step. Second category jump. Springing up from both feet, the working leg opens at the apex of the jump; the landing is onto one leg. It may travel *de côté*, *en arrière*, or *en avant*, or it may remain *en place*.

en avant

and   one
back leg opens in low *arabesque*

en arrière

and
front leg opens in low *devant*

one

à la seconde (changée)

(a) *Sissonne fermée.* Closed *sissonne.* The working leg closes fifth a moment after the landing has occurred.

(b) *Sissonne ouverte.* Open *sissonne.* The working leg remains extended *en l'air* after the landing has occurred. (The next step has to be a *temps levé.)* This can also be done with a *développé* into the open position, although the initial pushoff is still from both legs.

(c) *Sissonne sur les pointes.* The action is the same as for *sissonne sautée,* but instead of landing in a *demi-plié,* the movement is done with a spring onto *pointe,* then closes in fifth on *demi-plié.* The working leg may remain extended *en l'air,* in which case the next step must be a *relevé.*

Soubresaut. Sudden bound. First category jump. A spring upward from both feet to both feet. It can remain *en place* or travel *en avant, en arrière,* or *de côté.* The legs must be held close together throughout the action.

or   or   or

Sous-sus. Under-over. The name describes one foot being under, or in the back, and one foot being over, or in front. It is similar to a *soubresaut* but is done as a *relevé* onto both *pointes*.

Soutenu. Sustained. It can qualify a movement or refer to an actual step. From fifth position, the working leg slides out to *pointe tendue;* the supporting leg is in *demi-plié.* The working leg then joins the supporting one, both rising to half or full *pointe.* This can be done from any position.

(a) *Soutenu en tournant.* Sustained movement with a turn. The same actions are executed but with a *dégagé* to second position, adding a turn or swivel when both feet are together. The turn always occurs toward the back leg, the other leg coming forward to finish fifth position, either remaining on *demi-pointe* or dropping the heels into *demi-plié.* It can be done *en dehors,* the working leg closing back before the turn; or *en dedans,* the working leg closing front before the turn.

and   one

Temps de cuisses. Thigh movement. A compound step composed of a *retiré passé* and a *sissonne.* From a fifth position, right foot back, the right leg executes a low *retiré passé* while the left does a *demi-plié;* as soon as the right leg closes in fifth front, the dancer springs up with a *sissonne de côté*, closing front again. It may be executed in one or two counts.

and   one

Temps de flèche. Arrow step. Third category jump. Preceded by a *pas de bourrée couru* or a *glissade*, this is a high jump with one leg shooting through like an arrow. After a running preparation the left leg kicks in a *grand battement devant*, while the right leg pushes off and executes a *battement développé*. The landing occurs on the left leg with the right leg extended *devant*.

and   one   two

Temps levé. Lifting step. Third category jump. A hop on one leg, the other leg being in any desired position.

Temps liés. Linked movements. An exercise in the center which stresses coordination between arms and legs and uses a soft *demi-plié* to link the extensions. In its simpler form it is done with a *pointe tendue*, but in more advanced variations includes *en l'air* positions, the working leg being lifted to *attitude*, *arabesque*, or *seconde*. *Pirouettes* may also be included in the sequence. It is executed *en avant* with the working leg extending to *pointe tendue derrière* and then to *seconde*; and it can be done *en arrière* with the working leg extending to *pointe tendue devant* and then to *seconde*. With the right foot in front, fifth position, *dégagé devant* to fourth position *demi-plié* on both feet. The transfer of weight continues forward until the left leg stretches in *pointe tendue derrière* and the right leg is straight. Close fifth. *Dégagé* with the right leg again but to the side; *demi-plié* in second position; the weight transfers to the right leg while the left leg stretches to *pointe tendue*. Close fifth front, and repeat to the other side.

en avant

and   one   and

and *en arrière*

two   and   three   and

one   and   two

and   three

Temps de poisson. Step of the fish. Second category jump. An exaggerated *failli*. Leaping upward and slightly forward in *effacé* position in the air, the body curves back, legs held close together, like a fish jumping out of the water. The legs separate moments before the landing. The back leg finishes in *arabesque*, the front leg in *plié* bears the weight of the body. The back leg then swings forward through first position into a deep fourth with the weight of the body being transferred onto it.

and   one

Tombér. To fall. A fall onto one leg in *demi-plié*. Sometimes used in *adagio*, it can also be part of an *allegro enchaînement* as a link step or a preparation. It can be done in any direction.

from *devant*   from *à la seconde*

from *arabesque*

Tourner. To turn. Cecchetti's seventh basic movement of dancing.

Tours de rein. Turn with a highly arched back. Third category jump. A series of *grands jetés en avant* linked by a *coupé*. Often done *en manège*, the dancer leaps up, strongly arching the back; and, keeping the position of the *jeté*, revolves a full turn in the air. It may be performed either in *attitude* or in *arabesque*.

Tours en l'air. Turns in the air. The dancer springs up from both feet in fifth position and revolves one or more times, finishing in fifth position, opposite leg in front. *Tours en l'air* may also finish in various positions on one leg as well as on one knee.

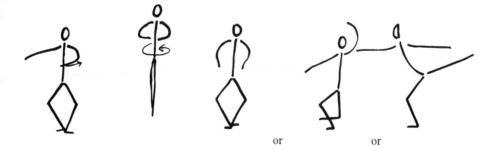

or   or

Selected Bibliography

Works Cited in the Text

Arbeau, Thoinot. *Orchesography: 15th and 16th Century Dances* (1588). Trans. Mary Stewart Evans. New York, Kamin Dance Publishers, 1948.

Baryshnikov at Work. Ed. Charles Engell France. New York, Alfred A. Knopf, 1976.

Beaumont, Cyril W., and Stanislas Idzikowski. *A Manual of the Theory and Practice of Classical Theatrical Dancing (Classical Ballet) (Cecchetti Method)*. London, C.W. Beaumont, 1922; reprinted various dates 1932–1971.

Blasis, Carlo. *Treatise upon the Theory and Practice of the Art of Dancing*. London, 1820; New York, Dover Books, 1968.

Boas, Franziska. *The Function of Dance in Human Society*. New York, Dance Horizons, 1944.

"A Conversation with P. W. Manchester." *Ballet Review*, vol. 6, no. 3 (1977–1978), pp. 57–89.

Daisetz Suzuki. *Zen and Japanese Culture*. Princeton, NJ, Princeton University Press, Bollinger Series, 1959.

Dolmetsch, Mabel. *Dances of England and France from 1450 to 1600* (1949). New York, Da Capo Press, Inc., 1975.

Fitt, Sally. *Dance Kinesiology*. New York, Schirmer Books, 1988.

Grant, J. C. B. *Grant's Atlas of Anatomy*. fifth edition. Baltimore, The Williams & Wilkins Co., 1962.

Gregory, John, and André Eglevsky. *Heritage of a Ballet Master: Nicolas Legat*. Foreword by Alexandra Danilova. New York, Dance Horizons, 1977.

Guilcher, Jean-Michel. *La Contradanse*. Paris, Mouton, 1969.

Laws, Kenneth. *The Physics of Dance*. New York, Schirmer Books, 1984.

Kirstein, Lincoln. *Ballet: Bias and Belief*. Pennington, NJ, Princeton Book Company, Publishers, 1983.

MacConaill, M. A., and J. V. Basmajian. *Muscles and Movements*. Baltimore, The Williams & Wilkins Co., 1969.

Noverre, Jean-Georges. *Letters on Dancing and Ballets* (1760). Trans. C. W. Beaumont, London, 1930; reprinted, New York, Dance Horizons, 1966.

Pavlova: A Biography. Ed. A.H. Franks. London, Burke Publishing Co. Ltd., 1956.

Robbins, Tom. *Another Roadside Attraction*. New York, Ballantine Books, 1971.

Roné, Elvira. *Olga Preobrazhenskaya: A Portrait*. Trans. and adapted by Fernau Hall. New York, Marcel Dekker, Inc., 1978.

Royce, Anya Peterson. *The Anthropology of Dance*. Bloomington, Indiana University Press, 1977.

Sachs, Curt. *World History of Dance*. New York, W. W. Norton & Co. Inc., 1937.

Sweigard, Lulu. *Human Movement Potential*. New York, Dodd, Mead and Co., 1974.

Todd, Mabel Elsworth. *The Hidden You*. New York, Exposition Press, 1953; reprinted, New York, Dance Horizons, 1976.

————. *The Thinking Body*. New York, Dance Horizons, 1953.

Vaganova, Agriopina. *Basic Principles of Classic Ballet: Russian Ballet Technique* (1934). Trans. Anatole Chujoy. New York, Kamin Dance Publishers, 1946; reprinted 1969.

Warren, Gretchen Ward. *Classical Ballet Technique*. Tampa, FL, 1989.

Warwick, R., and P. L. Williams. *Gray's Anatomy*. 35th British ed. Philadelphia, W. B. Saunders Co., 1973.

Wells, Katherine F., and Kathryn Luttgens. *Kinesiology: Scientific Basis of Human Motion*. Philadelphia: W. B. Saunders Co., 1976.

Works of Related Interest

Barringer, Janice, and Sarah Schlesinger. *The Pointe Book: Shoes, Training & Technique*. Pennington, NJ, Princeton Book Company, Publishers, 1990.

Berardi, Gigi. *Finding Balance: Fitness and Training for a Lifetime in Dance.* Pennington, NJ, Princeton Book Company, Publishers, 1991.

Biomechanical Studies of the Musculo-Skeletal System. Ed. F. Gaynor Evans. Springfield, Ill., Charles C. Thomas, 1961. A report of the Seventh International Congress of Anatomists, the work is especially informative on the composition of bones.

Bruhn, Erik, and Lillian Moore. *Bournonville and Ballet Technique.* London, Macmillan, 1961.

Clarke, Mary, and Clement Crisp. *Ballet: An Illustrated History.* New York, Universe Books, 1973.

Control of Posture and Locomotion. Ed. R. B. Stein et al. New York, Plenum Press, 1974. (Vol. 7 of *Advances in Behavioral Biology.*) Treats nearly all aspects of motor activity.

Dance as a Theatre Art: Source Readings in Dance History from 1581 to the Present. Ed. Selma Jeanne Cohen. New York, Dodd, Mead & Co.,1975,2nd Ed., Pennington, NJ, Princeton Book Company, Publishers, 1991.

Duchenne, G. B. *Physiology of Motion.* Trans. Emanuel B. Kaplan. Philadelphia, W. B. Saunders Co., 1959. A translation of the classic *Physiologie des Mouvements* (1867). Individual chapters discuss the action and use of muscles of the shoulder, upper arm, forearm, hand, thigh, leg, foot, respiratory system, and spine.

Ellfelt, Lois. *Dance: From Magic to Art.* Dubuque, Iowa, Wm. C. Brown Co., 1976.

Gelabert, Raoul. *Anatomy for the Dancer.* 2 volumes. New York, Dance Magazine, 1964.

Grant, Gail. *Technical Manual and Dictionary of Classical Ballet.* New York, Dover Books, 1967.

Kirstein, Lincoln. *Dance: A Short History of Classic Theatrical Dancing.* Pennington, NJ, Princeton Book Company, Publishers, 1988.

Koegler, Horst. *The Concise Oxford Dictionary of Ballet.* New York, Oxford University Press, 1977.

Lawson, Joan. *A History of Ballet and Its Makers.* London, Dance Books, 1973.

———. *Teaching Young Dancers: Muscular Co-ordination in Classical Ballet.* London, Adam & Charles Black, 1975. This book provides additional information on several points in my discussion (with some differences of opinion) and has a variety of illustrations that nicely supplement my own. Another work that appears to be relevant is Celia Sparger, *Anatomy and Ballet,* available from Adam & Charles Black, London.

Lowman, Charles L., and Cart H. Young. *Postural Fitness: Significance and Variances.* Philadelphia, Lea & Febiger, 1960. Treats musculoskeletal functions and malfunctions, with an analysis of common exercises.

Martin, John. *The Modern Dance*. New York, Dance Horizons, 1965.

Messerer, Asaf. *Classes in Classical Ballet*. Trans. Oleg Brianski. New York, Doubleday & Co., Inc., 1975.

Morton, Dudley J., and Dudley Dean Fuller. *Human Locomotion and Body Form: A Study of Gravity and Man*. Baltimore, The Williams & Wilkins Co., 1952. Especially good on the mobility and actions of the feet.

Prunières, Henri. *Le Ballet du Cour en France avant Benserade et Lully*. Paris, H. Laurens, 1914.

Roslavleva, Natalia. *Era of the Russian Ballet*. New York, E. P. Dutton & Co., Inc., 1966.

Thompson, Clem W. *Manual of Structural Kinesiology*. St. Louis, C. V. Mosby Co., 1977. Contains numerous excellent illustrations of the bones and muscles of all major joints.

Vincent, L. M., M.D. *The Dancer's Book of Health*. Kansas City, Sheed Andrews & McMeel, 1978, reprinted, Pennington, NJ, Princeton Book Company, Publishers, 1988.

Watkins, Andrea, and Priscilla M. Clarkson. *Dancing Longer, Dancing Stronger: A Dancer's Guide to Improving Technique and Preventing Injury*. Pennington, NJ, Princeton Book Company, Publishers, 1990.

Index